# SKETCH OF RAILWAY NETWORK OF

# METRO-LAND

' A GLORIOUS UNSPOILED
COUNTRYSIDE, SITUATED
IN MIDDLESEX, HERTS
AND BUCKS, EASILY AND
QUICKLY REACHED BY THE
METROPOLITAN RAILWAY '

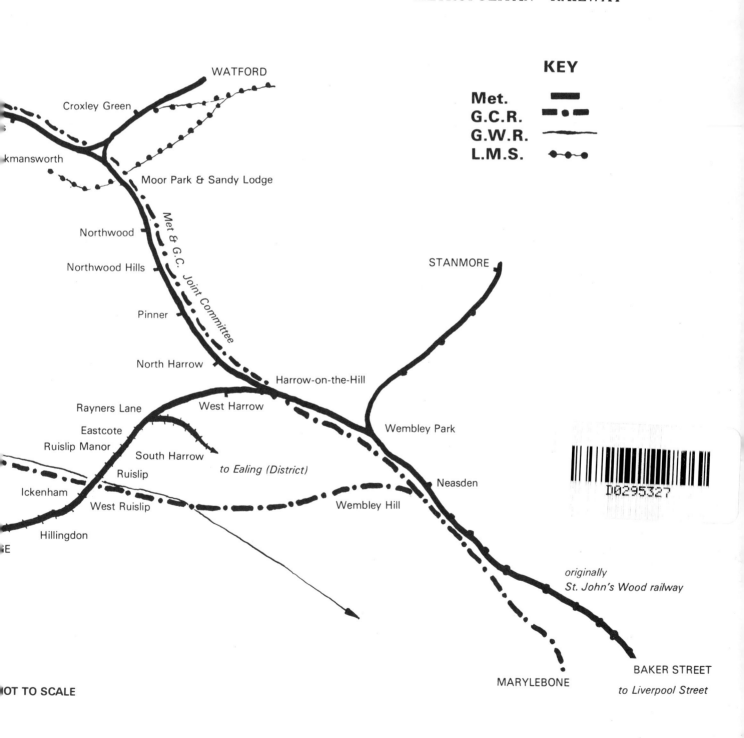

**KEY**

Met.
G.C.R.
G.W.R.
L.M.S.

WATFORD

Croxley Green

kmansworth

Moor Park & Sandy Lodge

Met & G.C. Joint Committee

Northwood

Northwood Hills

STANMORE

Pinner

North Harrow

Harrow-on-the-Hill

Rayners Lane          West Harrow

Eastcote

Ruislip Manor                           Wembley Park

South Harrow

to Ealing (District)

Ruislip

Ickenham                                    Neasden

West Ruislip          Wembley Hill

Hillingdon

E

originally
St. John's Wood railway

MARYLEBONE          BAKER STREET

OT TO SCALE                            to Liverpool Street

# METRO MEMORIES

Forget the depression; forget the dole queue; leave London's dust and bustle behind you and get to the sunny side of the street. Pack the picnic hamper, fill the Thermos flask, put a film in the 'Brownie' camera and off to Baker Street and the train out into Metro-land.

# METRO MEMORIES

*An armchair odyssey through the
countryside served by the
Metropolitan Railway*

by
Dennis Edwards
and
Ron Pigram

BLOOMSBURY BOOKS
LONDON

This book is dedicated with affection to all members of that
exclusive 'club' – the former employees of the Metropolitan
Railway, including the father of one of the authors.

First published in 1977 by Midas Books

Reprinted in 1985 by
BATON TRANSPORT
1 Russell Chambers,
Covent Garden, London, WC2E 8AA

© Dennis F. Edwards and Ron Pigram, 1977

This edition published 1988 by
Bloomsbury Books an imprint of
Godfrey Cave Associates Limited
42 Bloomsbury Street London WC1B 3QJ
under license from Baton Transport/Cleveland Press

ISBN 1 870630 95 5

Printed in Yugoslavia

# CONTENTS

# ACKNOWLEDGMENTS

The authors wish to acknowledge the help given by Charles E. Lee, F.C.I.T., H.C. Casserley and C.R.L. Coles (who lent pictures from their collections), and the many others who have helped — especially the librarians at the reference libraries at Brent and Hillingdon as well as the curator of Aylesbury County Museum. We wish particularly to acknowledge R. Bosher and R. Crouch for their help in copying so many of the rarer pictures, and E. Sigrist for unfolding memories of railway working near the turn of the century.

Cover design by Vince Power
*Front cover:* An H Class engine of 1920 with 'Dreadnought' carriages near Chorleywood in the 1930s.

*Back cover:* New building in Metro-land mid-1930s.

*Endpapers:* Map of Metro-land.

*Contents page:* Moor Park station with old timber platform.

## THE AUTHORS

*Ron Pigram* is the author of a number of books on the Chilterns. He is a Member of the Chartered Institute of Transport and has lectured for some years on the history and topography of the region. He admits that the pleasure of walking in the Chilterns, which he first experienced as a child in Metro-land, is so great that he can never be free from its spell. He is a member of the London Transport Group of Artists, and exhibits regularly at the Royal Exchange in London.

*Dennis F. Edwards* was born in a typical suburban 'semi' in Metro-land. Now in his 40s, with a wife and young daughter, he lives within sound of the railway on the Uxbridge Line. He is a confirmed environmentologist, and is Publicity Officer for a local Civic Trust Group. He has also written a number of local history and walks books.

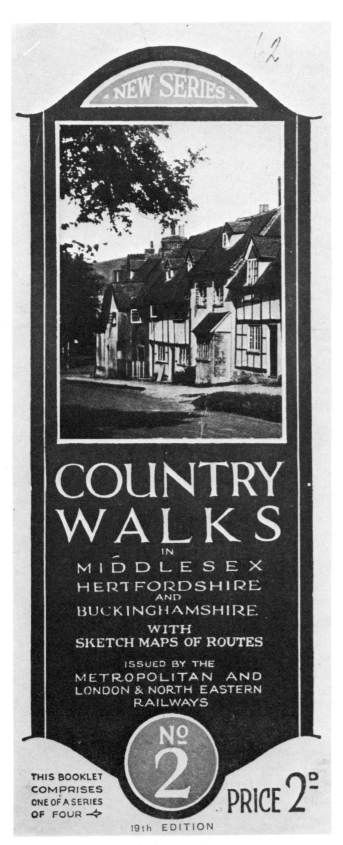

Metropolitan Railway walking books were always popular with Londoners and did much to acquaint them with the country life offered by living in Metro-land. This edition, which dates from about 1924, had upright sketch maps, and each walk was condensed into the length of a page.

Photograph: Authors' Collection

'METRO-LAND' . . . The Metropolitan Railway is issuing an attractive handbook bearing the above title, by which the company has named the districts served by its system. Half an hour from Baker Street by fast train takes you into the heart of 'Metro-land', into charming country yet unspoiled, wherein is some of the most exquisite rural scenery to be found in England.

*Railway Gazette* 23 July 1915

The song of the nightingale for which the neighbourhood is renowned; its mingled pastures, woods and streams; its gentle hills clothed with verdure; the network of translucent rivers traversing the peaceful valley render it a Mecca to the City man pining for country and pure air.

Early *Metro-land* guide

## THE METROPOLITAN RAILWAY
### Baker Street Station Buffet

Early Electric! With what radiant hope
  Men formed this many-branched electrolier,
Twisted the flex around the iron rope
  And let the dazzling vacuum globes hang clear,
And then with hearts the rich contrivance fill'd
Of copper, beaten by the Bromsgrove Guild.

Early Electric! Sit you down and see,
  'Mid this fine woodwork and a smell of dinner,
A stained-glass windmill and a pot of tea,
  And Sepia views of leafy lanes in PINNER, —
Then visualise, far down the shining lines,
Your parents' homestead set in murmuring pines.

Smoothly from HARROW, passing PRESTON ROAD,
  They saw the last green fields and misty sky,
At NEASDEN watched the workmen's train unload,
  And, with the morning villas sliding by,
They felt so sure on their electric trip
That Youth and Progress were in partnership.

And all that day in murky London Wall
  The thought of RUISLIP kept him warm inside;
At FARRINGDON that lunch hour at a stall
  He bought a dozen plants of London Pride;
While she, in arc-lit Oxford Street adrift,
Soared through the sales by safe hydraulic lift.

Early Electric! Maybe even here
  They met that evening at six-fifteen
Beneath the hearts of this electrolier
  And caught the first non-stop to WILLESDEN GREEN
Then out and on, through rural RAYNERS LANE
To autumn-scented Middlesex again.

Cancer has killed him. Heart is killing her.
  The trees are down. An Odeon flashes fire
Where stood their villa by the murmuring fir
  When "they would for children's good conspire,"
Of all their loves and hopes on hurrying feet
Thou art the worn memorial, Baker Street.

**Reproduced by kind permission of
Sir John Betjeman**

From *Collected Poems*
published by John Murray Limited

'Hikers' take a rest with the help of a Met brake van at Great Missenden
(or perhaps Wendover). The date is the early 1930s. The ends of the van
were painted crimson.

Photograph: Authors' Collection

# INTRODUCTION

This book takes you on a nostalgic journey north-west from London into 'Metro-land'. It is not a technical railway history but makes a journey back in time, with the aid of contemporary photographs, re-creating the charm and excitement of those long lost days in Middlesex, Hertfordshire and Buckinghamshire between the 1890s and the mid-1930s.

This is a journey which begins beneath the bulk of Chiltern Court at Baker Street, then travels out to Wembley Park, where Metro-land really begins, and along the flat lands to Harrow and its hill and down memory lane to those Sunday School treats of long ago at Eastcote and Ruislip. Here the housing estates began and the Londoner was tempted to come out and make a new life in the country in a well-designed house amid the fresh fields and woods.

Further on we reach Pinner and Northwood, with their large villas amid the trees, and then pass exclusive Moor Park and the golf courses and so come across the water meadows to Rickmansworth and Watford. Now we climb through the Chilterns, perhaps with memories of country walks, horse rides, picnics and beech woods, and on to the Vale of Aylesbury and rural places such as Quainton Road and Brill, lost in the fields of an unchanged England. The journey ends at Verney Junction, where nobody ever seemed to go — or even change trains!

69

# COUNTRY WALKS.

◆━◆━◆

TO those fond of walking who appreciate open, bracing air, the directions given in the few specimen country rambles with which the Guide has this season been supplemented will probably be welcomed.

The walks, particulars of which are given below, have been personally undertaken and followed, and all unnecessary details have been omitted in the directions, the simple object being to enable the walker to enjoy an exhilarating ramble in a district with which he may not be familiar, satisfied in the possession of complete particulars of the route.

The routes are not confined to highways, but are varied by taking the pedestrian through fields, meadows, and woods.

━━◆━━

## Rickmansworth to Sarratt and back.

Bear to the right on leaving Rickmansworth Station, and pass under the railway bridge to a path through posts on the left. Then in a few yards cross by a bridge over the railway and road into Rickmansworth Park. Take footpath to the left, slanting towards a fine avenue, to where it runs out into the main road. Turn to the right for a quarter of a mile, and take the first road to the right. At the foot of the hill, and just before reaching a house, take a path through a white gate on the left, and continue along the enclosed path. Where it forks—in a quarter of a mile—keep along the level by the side of a fence, crossing a private road to a house, and continue through the meadows to a stile by the side of a clump of fir trees. Thence cross a field into a road, where turn twenty yards to the left, and take a footpath to the right through two fields into an enclosed green strip planted with young trees. Cross the white footbridge over the River Chess, and take the path that leaves the level ground and slants upwards to a road, where turn to the right and continue up hill a quarter of a mile to Church End.

Pass through the churchyard, taking the path to the right, which commands a fine woodland view across the valley of the

F

The first Metropolitan country walks, in the handbook issued by the Met in 1904. The idea quickly proved very popular and became an established part of Metro-land life.

## METRO-LAND . . . WHERE THE WILD FLOWERS GROW

The image of Metro-land is as identifiable with the period between the two world wars as char-a-bancs, school treats and jazz. To most people who lived around London in those days it meant many things — most of them associated with the countryside and fresh air — and was so intense that Metro-land has come to us, almost fifty years on, as more than nostalgia.

The term 'Metro-land' came into use as a means of promoting passenger traffic to that part of Middlesex, the Buckinghamshire Chilterns and the Vale of Aylesbury through which the Metropolitan Railway had built its lines. Considerable research has been done into the first use of the word, but no definite date has been discovered. The historian Charles E. Lee gives the general date as spring 1915.

In later years the large and colourful ubiquitous publicity booklets of the Metropolitan Railway were built around the word. During the 1920s and 1930s many campaigns were launched by railway companies to persuade Londoners to abandon the friendly grime of their tiny flats and live in the nearby countryside. Any extension of London's Underground railways was followed by the mushroom growth of thousands of new homes, all looking very much alike. The railways of that time had been grouped within the general framework of the 'Underground', but until the London Passenger Transport Board was formed in 1933 the Metropolitan Railway, with its London lines to New Cross and to Hammersmith (the latter operated under a joint committee with the Great Western Railway) as well as its 'extension' line to Verney Junction, was in a different position from the rest of the railways serving the capital. In its early years, the Metropolitan was intended to be a 'terminal railway' as well as a local line, taking Great Western, Great Northern and Midland trains through to the City of London and also on to the London, Chatham Dover Railway to the south. Since the 1870s, however, the Metropolitan Railway had regarded itself as a main-line company; even in the early 1920s, the railway sought to re-assert that image in the face of the main-line amalgamations that were undertaken at that time.

The second reason why the Metropolitan was different was because of the vast surplus lands which it owned and which had done so much to make the Metropolitan's dividends so consistently good. The Metropolitan Railway Estate Company therefore built new homes for Londoners along its tracks. The houses were aimed at the middle classes and were carefully controlled in design and number. To own a house in Metro-land was a status symbol. From their windows of leaded diamond panes and their fancifully-illuminated doors incorporating glass that tinged the sun's rays with blues, apple greens and yellows, the fortunate owners looked over a fresh faerie-land, sweet-smelling and very much like the land of Lionel Monckton's Edwardian musical comedies.

Gradually the new estates started to appear — close to London at first, for there was still plenty of land available only a few miles out from Baker Street. City clerks, tradesmen and others who had a steady income in the uncertain years of the 1920s were hurried out to see the house of their dreams, many developers meeting prospective customers in black 'motor-cars' which avoided at least some of the mud and slosh of the site. Further out of Town, and within easy reach of a restful round of golf, estates of more elegant homes were created. These had more bedrooms, were architect-designed and were often wreathed with mature trees to give an embosked sense of completeness with the new country life their owners wished to enjoy. The fragile young saplings planted in rows on the more densely-built estates, the box-like wooden fencing and the unmade roads were not for the wealthier class. Even the new craze of the cinema hardly appealed — for these people the real joy in life was to stretch out in 'plus-fours' or to try out the new dances after a week of life in the counting houses of the City.

So arose a new stratified society of the lower-middle class with a secure enough income to satisfy the very easy requirements of a building society, the managerial class who moved into the country estates of Metro-land and the old country gentry who travelled up to Town for a few days each week but kept their hearts firmly on the pleasures of following the hounds. The Metropolitan Railway linked all these people together, and its magenta-coloured locomotives pulled them into London and out again. This was one of the first of London's commuter societies, although the word had not yet come into use and the men in their moquette-covered seats would not have understood that they were making history.

For others not so fortunate and still anchored to London's smoke and noise the Metropolitan Railway promoted to very good effect the delights of a day in Metro-land by fast electric train. It was an attractive idea, and in spite of the general economic depression at the end of the 1920s the Metro-land spirit and all it stood for was to become one of the most attractive and colourful of the developments of London's suburbia.

The poets reflected this need, felt by many, to get away from the dirt and bustle of London streets, fouled by horses and swarming with flies, which thrived in spite of 'fly-papers' covered with the bodies of trapped insects in most food-shops. The life of the Chiltern fields and meadows spurred poets and writers, sensitive to the mood of the times. George R. Sims, writing during the carnage of the First World War, made one of the earliest references to Metro-land in verse.

> I know a land where the wild flowers grow,
> Near, near at hand if by train you go,
> 'Metro-land', 'Metro-land',
> Meadows sweet have a golden glow,
> Hills are green as the vales below
> In 'Metro-land', 'Metro-land'.
>
> 'Metro-land', 'Metro-land',
> Leafy dell and woodland fair,
> Land of love and hope and peace;
> Land where all your troubles cease –
> 'Metro-land', 'Metro-land',
> Waft, oh waft me there;
> Hearts are lighter, eyes are brighter
> In 'Metro-land', 'Metro-land'.

What sort of countryside did the new adventurers find as they stood to get their bearings on the heavily-creosoted platforms of the country stations, with the coloured enamelled-iron signs and advertisement boards? This book shows something of life in Metro-land, with very special and rightly reverent comment on the beloved railway that made it all possible.

## THE VISION OF SIR EDWARD
It is still true to claim that Metro-land received its first real kiss of life through the bewhiskered lips of that stubborn old knight, Sir Edward Watkin. He was one of the toughest of all the Victorian tycoons, way back in the 1870s. This story of Metro-land is not a detailed examination of nineteenth-century railways, but it is useful to take a general look, as the borders of

Metropolitan Railway territory could have been very different from the final outer limits of Verney Junction (only five miles or so from Buckingham) and Brill, on the borders of Oxfordshire.

The Metropolitan was the world's first underground urban railway. It opened between Paddington and Farringdon Street in 1863. The tiny seed that was to grow into the main line of the Metropolitan Railway was planted as early as 1864, with proposals for a Baker Street & St. John's Wood Railway, a semi-independent company in which the Met had a large shareholding. This line was to link up with the Hampstead Junction Railway near Finchley Road. The new line was built as a single track branch with double lines at the stations, but the money ran out and Swiss Cottage became the terminus. The St. John's Wood Railway did not become part of the Metropolitan officially until 1 January 1883.

Sir Edward Watkin was nominated Chairman of the Metropolitan Railway on 7 August 1872 (effective from October of that year), and it was under his direction that the line aspired to main-line greatness. For the next twenty-two years, Watkin played his political cards so close to his chest that even today there lurks doubt about his intentions, although he was known to have cosseted the idea of a grand trunk railway route from the Midlands and the North to Dover by way of the Manchester, Sheffield & Lincolnshire Railway (which was destined to expand southwards and open its London terminus at Marylebone and to be renamed Great Central), the Metropolitan and the South Eastern Railway. Sir Edward was Chairman of the Channel Tunnel Company — so here was a vision of a great iron trade link with Europe.

Watkin was not a major shareholder in the Metropolitan, and his invitation to take the chair came at that time because of his experience — 'as a physician might be called to an ailing person,' as one observer put it. He was already chairman of the M.S. & L. and the South Eastern. The Met was in poor financial shape, and at that time the only northward extension was the single-tracked branch to Swiss Cottage mentioned earlier. Watkin made a fresh start: 'I have the resignations of all the Board in my hands,' he told a shareholders' meeting in October 1872. Watkin was determined that the Metropolitan 'would break through the iron barrier which the skill and acuteness of the larger railway companies have constructed around it'.

The Wotton Tramway, laid down as a light railway by the Duke of Buckingham and later to become part of the Metropolitan system, had been finished in 1872. Another of the Duke's creations, the Aylesbury & Buckingham Railway, ran as a local line, worked by the Great Western, from Aylesbury to Verney Junction (with a connection to the London & North Western Railway) by way of Quainton Road. Watkin, who saw the usefulness of the Aylesbury & Buckingham Railway in his long-term plans, was cautious with his Metropolitan shareholders, knowing that they were more interested in developing the market value of their shares than in new lines. But in 1874, under guise of concern about the low percentage of goods traffic carried by the Metropolitan, Watkin spoke of profits coming from north of London and sought to extend the Metropolitan to Harrow, using the tiny St. John's Wood railway. At Harrow, he said, 'lines under the control of the Duke of Buckingham have been sanctioned down to Rickmansworth' and would lie within reach of a further northward extension. Sir Edward's concluding remarks — 'When the Metropolitan reaches Harrow it becomes part of a new system extending all the way to Buckingham, and there are disjointed pieces of railway which will help to connect the Metropolitan's termini with Northampton, Birmingham and other large towns' — generally skimmed over the heads of those present, who were more concerned with finding objections to a proposed Metropolitan Railway Hotel at Moorgate Street. Almost unnoticed too were his comments about 'further powers being applied for'. Watkin did not refresh the memories of the Metropolitan shareholders, for he considered that they had silently acquiesced, and turned to discussing railway matters with the Duke of Buckingham, who was very interested in using railways to bring his estate produce to town. Agreement between the two resulted in the 1874 Acts for the Harrow & Rickmansworth Railway and the Kingsbury & Harrow Railway. In the next year power was sought to build north to Aylesbury. It seems unlikely that at this time Watkin had any definite idea of the route which his company's northward expansion would take to reach the Midlands, for the Manchester, Sheffield & Lincolnshire Railway had not yet made any attempt to build southwards.

The Duke of Buckingham had seen that there were a number of options open beyond Aylesbury in the heart of his estates and had no doubt discussed them with Watkin. In a letter of 20 September 1873 to John Aird, a contractor, the Duke discussed a link between a railway from Aylesbury to London and his own Aylesbury & Buckingham line to Verney Junction, which would then run over the L. & N.W. metals to Buckingham, with a prospect of continuing north from there. Another idea ventilated in this letter was to extend the Wotton Tramway from Brill to Oxford, a distance of ten miles. Considerable attention was given to this link to Oxford. Had either of these ideas left the ground, the Metropolitan's country extension lines of the 1900s might well have developed into main lines. It was not to be. So, gently, the Verney Junction line (which had been double-tracked upon the arrival of the Metropolitan Railway at Aylesbury in January 1894) sank back to become almost a branch line. The Brill branch remained just a branch and so helped to create the sylvan scene successfully built up over the years as Metro-land by Metropolitan Railway publicity.

## WATKIN AND THE MANCHESTER, SHEFFIELD & LINCOLNSHIRE RAILWAY

Not until 1890, after an agreement for through bookings and the interchange of traffic was already in force between the Metropolitan, the M.S. & L. Railway and the South Eastern Railway, did Watkin emerge into the open at a Metropolitan shareholders' meeting. Thumping his hand against a large wall map he shouted, 'Do you see that red line? That tells the whole story.' Parliament had agreed to the M.S. & L. Railway's extension southwards to the Midlands to Aylesbury and to the Met's extension northwards to Aylesbury. 'And we have an agreement with the Aylesbury & Buckingham Railway to take the line further north again,' he added. At about this time he told Gladstone that he hoped to have the 'privilege of running you in a train from Hawarden to Dover'.

Watkin invited the shareholders to adopt an agreement with the M.S. & L. Railway which gave running powers over the Metropolitan Railway's extension from Quainton Road to Baker Street — a distance of forty-two miles. This agreement, which gave a third of the total receipts to the M.S. & L. Railway and two-thirds to the Met, was to form a basis of smouldering resentment over the years ahead, as the M.S. & L. Railway built its London extension. That story lies outside the scope of this book, however. As a result of Watkin's arrangements, the Metropolitan Railway was pushed northward in stages from Harrow to Rickmansworth and Chesham and then

from Amersham on to Aylesbury. The first Metropolitan through service between Baker Street and Verney Junction began on 1 January 1897, the Brill branch becoming part of the system under lease in 1899. The railway service to Metro-land was complete.

## LATER DAYS ON THE METROPOLITAN
Sir Edward Watkin had to retire through ill health in 1894 and died shortly afterwards. Under John Bell, his successor, the Metropolitan was less concerned with grandiose expansion. The Great Central Railway settled down after the opening of the terminus at Marylebone (separate tracks were provided south of Harrow) and more peaceful days arrived.

The next Metropolitan extension was in Middlesex: the Harrow & Uxbridge Railway. There had been a number of schemes for railways to open up the rural districts west of Harrow, including a London & South Wales Railway, which would have been a threat to the G.W.R. With the proposals for the G.W.R. and G.C.R. joint line between South Ruislip (Northolt Junction) and High Wycombe and beyond, the District sought powers to extend its projected Ealing & Harrow line to Uxbridge. Eventually, the Harrow & Uxbridge Railway received approval in 1897. The objective of the new line was to link the District Railway's Ealing & South Harrow line with the Metropolitan. The final plan included the construction of a link from Harrow to Rayners Lane with a branch to South Harrow. In the end, the Metropolitan (Harrow & Uxbridge Railway) opened the line through from Harrow to Uxbridge, but the South Harrow link was not used until District trains began running through to Rayners Lane and Uxbridge in 1910. The Metropolitan branch to Uxbridge opened in 1904 and was built for electric traction, although steam services were operated until 1905. With the electrification of the line from Baker Street to Harrow and Uxbridge, traffic greatly increased. On the 'main' line electric locomotives had taken the Aylesbury trains first as far as Willesden Green, and later to Wembley, then to Harrow and from 1925 to Rickmansworth, from where they were taken to the Chilterns by steam locomotive.

After the First World War two more branches were built to open up the country for housing developments — the Watford branch in 1925 and the Stanmore branch in 1932.

The Metropolitan Railway was unique among railway companies in that it was empowered to grant building licences and sell ground rents in the City of London. In 1887 the Metropolitan Surplus Lands Committee was formed to acquire areas of land adjacent to the line. In 1912, Robert H. Selbie, the Company Secretary, suggested the formation of a separate company to develop the land, since he thought that the Committee was not obtaining a proper benefit from the land. Eventually, on 7 June 1919, the Metropolitan Railway Estates Company was set up with a capital of £150,000. It was a highly successful enterprise, and by the outbreak of the Second World War some 4,600 homes had been built.

The Brill branch closed in 1935, the passenger services to Verney in 1936 and the freight traffic, with the larger steam locomotives, was transferred to the L.N.E.R. in 1937. After the extension of electric traction to Amersham in 1961, the services to Aylesbury were operated by British Rail.

At the peak of its existence in 1932, the Metropolitan had a route mileage of ninety-eight and carried 109,562,000 passengers (including 63,263 season-ticket holders). Freight traffic consisted of 1,015,501 tons of general merchandise, 662,764 tons of coal, 2,478,212 tons of minerals and 25,216 tons of livestock. Rolling stock was made up of 104 steam carriages and 544 goods vehicles, plus 100 service vehicles. Electric stock numbered 603 motor cars and trailers, 36 steam locomotives, 21 electric locomotives (including the Great Northern and City tube shunter). The railway also built for its staff 303 houses and had 591 houses for sale, 33 motor vehicles and 42 horse-drawn vans.

The Metropolitan Railway had always been strongly opposed to the formation of the London Passenger Transport Board in 1933, and on the last day of its existence as a separate company it is said that Lord Aberconway, his fellow-directors and staff brought most of the old company's papers out of the Baker Street offices and made a ceremonial bonfire of the lot. As the flames licked upwards, they marked the end of a dream and a whole page of English transport history.

## A JOURNEY BY TRAIN

Metro-land journeys began at the long, curving platforms of Baker Street. In Metropolitan Railway days there were three intermediate stations along the tunnel section to Finchley Road: St. John's Wood (later Lord's), Marlborough Road and Swiss Cottage. The stations were closed when the Bakerloo tube was opened beneath the Met lines in 1938, although Lord's survived until 1939. They were three stations where few people ever seemed to alight.

Finchley Road marks the end of the tunnel section. The station was originally a two-platform affair (1879), but it was remodelled with an island platform in 1913 and rebuilt again in 1938 with two islands. From Finchley Road to West Hampstead the Metropolitan goods yards could be seen on the right and then, after West Hampstead, the rooftops of Kilburn and the Edgware Road as the line runs on a viaduct.

The suburbs of pre-First World War London only reached as far as Dollis Hill, with the exception of some isolated developments near the old Kingsbury station (now Neasden). Here the train passed through the brick arches of the old Dog Lane bridge and soon, on the right, the wide spread of the Metropolitan Railway's works and the power station could be seen. There was always something of interest here: new rolling stock, experimental carriages — or just ancient vehicles awaiting the breaker. After crossing the River Brent (which flows down from the Welsh Harp reservoir) the traveller came to the new houses of the Chalk Hill estate — the real start of Metro-land. At Wembley, until its removal in 1907, the stump of Watkin's Folly — the abortive Wembley Tower — could be seen above the trees. In 1924 and 1925 the British Empire Exhibition was held on the site and the world-famous stadium was built. Wembley Park is still the busiest station on the line when important events such as the Cup Final are held.

Beyond Wembley, the quiet Middlesex countryside began. The Metropolitan branch to Stanmore curved round the flank of Barn Hill to Kingsbury and Canons The Stanmore branch became part of the Bakerloo Line when the tube was extended from Baker Street in 1939.

Preston Road station was originally on the Wembley side of the Preston Lane bridge but was rebuilt on its present site in 1931. Just after this bridge the land of the Harrow Golf Club ran along the left-hand side of the line as it climbed towards Northwick Park with its fine views of Harrow Hill. In later days there was another golf course here at Northwick Park, just beyond the L.M.S. main line.

At Harrow-on-the-Hill the train might be invaded by crowds of schoolchildren, for the town was famous for its large number of private educational establishments. The big white-and-red enamel signs on the station proclaimed

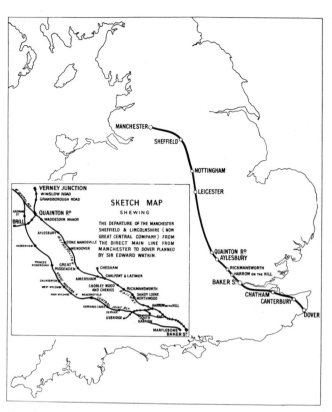

Map showing the link Sir Edward Watkin planned between Manchester and Dover via Aylesbury and the Metropolitan Railway.

'Junction for Eastcote, Ruislip and Uxbridge'. The line to Uxbridge left the main railway by a burrowing junction and curved round to West Harrow, with its rows of red-brick Edwardian houses and streets named after famous headmasters of Harrow School. Flat meadows came next, and then the junction with the District Railway at Rayners Lane. There was little here except fields and grazing sheep until about 1930, when the first housing estate was laid out on Worple Way and High Worple to the left of the line. Later came the Metropolitan's Harrow Garden Village Estate on the Pinner side.

Many were the pairs of small feet that trod the platforms of Eastcote; excited children pushed up the inclined approaches to the Field End Road on their way to the delights of the donkey Derby and the amusements at 'The Pavilion'.

A shallow cutting ran to Ruislip Manor, where there were only flat fields reaching southwards until Mr T.F. Nash and his builders arrived in the early 1930s. Ruislip goods yard lay between the Manor station and Ruislip, the only intermediate station building of substance. It had (and still retains) a typical Metropolitan lattice-style footbridge. Ruislip was the first large village on the line from Harrow. Here were an ancient church, a manor house, woodlands and a lake, plus a number of places for refreshments. It was always a popular spot for visitors to Metro-land.

The line passed on under the G.W.R. and G.C.R. line to High Wycombe and the RAF buildings on the right. To the left the countryside has largely remained unspoiled. The halt at Ickenham, with its corrugated iron waiting huts and tiny ticket office on the road above (you stood on the pavement to book your ticket), remained the same until 1971 — the last of the old Metropolitan halts. Down the lane from the halt slumbered the tiny village with its picturesque pond, ornamental pump and church. To the north-west of the village the great Jacobean mansion of Swakeleys lay amid its wooded grounds. Until the end of the First World War it was the home of the Gilbey family (the vintners), and Arthur Gilbey was a familiar figure as he drove his coach and pair along the local lanes.

Hillingdon station was opened between Ickenham and Uxbridge in 1923 to serve the Swakeleys estate developments and also the Metropolitan's new estates down the road towards Hillingdon village.

Finally, the line passed through a deep cutting to the goods yards and passenger terminus in Belmont Road, Uxbridge. Here the building was very similar to that at Ruislip. Between the wars, Uxbridge was a country town in transition: electric trams ran through to Shepherd's Bush, country people came into the market and buses ran to the villages of Buckinghamshire. There were also the G.W.R. termini at High Street (for Denham) and Vine Street (for West Drayton).

If we return to the main line, North Harrow station marked the end of the pre-1914 development of Harrow and the beginning of the wooded countryside around Pinner. In the 1920s, however, the area began to be developed, and soon North Harrow acquired rows of semi-detached houses and a cinema. Pinner was one of the most attractive places along the line, and it has retained its ancient village street and old buildings to this day. The parish church has a very prominent clock and the old Great Central locomotive men used to check their running time as they passed along the line. Pinner had many old farms, orchards and cottages, as well as fine villas tucked away amid its leafy lanes.

Northwood Hills was one of the very last stations opened on the old Metropolitan Railway, and its name is said to have been coined as a result of a competition organized by the Company. Certainly there was very little other than fields in this rather open landscape before the railways built a stopping-place there to serve brave new suburbia. Fields stretched on all the way to Northwood until the early 1930s. Northwood was a suburb of quality, the periphery of the more well-to-do rail traveller. Here stood avenues with mature trees, gravel drives and dark red-brick houses, shrubberies and tennis courts. Nannies moved purposefully along the stately shopping parade of Green Lane, pushing high black prams and standing no nonsense from the children.

The change from suburbia to the country life seemed to occur quietly as the trains slid to a half beside the heavily-built timber platforms of Moor Park & Sandy Lodge. Like the track itself, the wood was heavy with preservative and its dark, mellow tones seemed to blend with the green mask of trees near the track. The station had started life as Sandy Lodge but by Metro-land days had acquired the longer Moor Park & Sandy Lodge. The name was altered again, on 25 September 1950, when it became just Moor Park. If Moor Park mansion can be said to be the grandest eighteenth-century mansion in Hertfordshire, the station was to become the most exclusive place on the line. Here were houses so exclusive that even the roads were gated and private. The great Moor Park Mansion built for Benjamin Styles, a merchant who had made a fortune out of the South Sea Bubble, stands nearby. Its lawns became one of London's premier golf courses — a great consideration, of course, in Metro-land days. Classical gods and putti trail garlands from Moor Park's intricate ceilings, usually to the complete disregard of the club members taking tea below. Moor Park became the City man's dream!

A branch was laid to Watford in 1924, once again to develop estates. The line curves deeply through the chalk, running through the rather gloomy station at Croxley Green and so to Watford. The railway stopped short of the town at a villa-style terminus that hides shyly in a quiet side road near Cassiobury Park. Outside, the Metropolitan 'bus would wait to take you up to Watford High Street and the delights of The Empress Restaurant and the Palm Court Trio!

From Moor Park to Rickmansworth the main line crossed the Grand Union Canal and the River Colne and the single-track L.M.S. branch to Rickmansworth Church Street. At Rickmansworth outer Metro-land began.

## ONWARDS, BY STEAM

The locomotive changes at Rickmansworth took place from 1925 until the end of steam in 1961. Throughout these years the 4-minute interval at the station (3 minutes only were allowed in early days) while the Metropolitan Vickers electric locomotive was exchanged for the duty steam locomotive were moments as exciting and packed with bustle as the interval in a cinema show! The duty steam locomotive was usually waiting at the north end, and the electric one would scurry back on the 'up' road, slipping into the far siding and ready for the next 'up' train to London.

Black smuts, bursts of oily steam and whistles broke into the carriages (the old brown-painted compartment stock). Reconnected, the train pulled away. Past the new houses of the Cedars Estate built by the Metropolitan Estates, the train wound northwards to Chorley Wood and its common of fern and furzes. Away to the right ran the Chess valley — the shallow stream flecked with watercress beds, paddling cattle and the odd strand of barbed wire near the water, a scene so beloved of Metropolitan Railway literature.

At Chalfont & Latimer (Chalfont Road until 1916) there were many paths leading down to the Chess and up to the hill-top village of Chenies, with its great house belonging to the Russell family (the Dukes of Bedford), and to the sister hamlet of Latimer down beside the Chess. This borderland country between Buckinghamshire and Hertfordshire is heavy with history. In the water meadows once stood old Flaunden church, almost unapproachable in bad weather and lucky to have the services of a curate from Bovingdon twice a month. Small wonder that the church-loving Victorians were glad to see a new church from the young Gilbert Scott built on a more convenient site and pleased also to let the old church tumble into ruin. A few crumbling remnants can still be found. Nearby in the low-lying meadows of the Chess stands the lonely tomb of William Liberty, an eighteenth-century 'freethinker' who preferred to do any celestial contemplation away from the crowds. Chalfont & Latimer station is the junction for the Chesham branch, the last branch line before Aylesbury. This single line still survives and was electrified many years after the disappearance of the Metropolitan Railway, in 1961. It worked as a 'push-pull' shuttle. In Metropolitan Railway days the push-pull service was provided by unusual bogie coaches known as the Ashbury stock, which were purchased many years later by the Bluebell Railway. The Ashbury bogie stock trains had been equipped many years earlier for electric traction. The 'Dreadnought' carriages, reserved for use on the Chesham shuttle, were needed for the increase of steam trains from five to six carriages and the Ashbury stock filled the Chesham branch requirements.

Chesham station, well placed near the centre of the town, is reached by a series of rather tight curves.

Amersham, the next station northwards, stands on a steep hill well away from the market town in the valley of the river Misbourne, a tiny stream that during some summers 'disappears' under the chalk. In the years before the Second World War this was seen by some locals as a clear portent of troubled times that were to come. After

## THE HUNTING SEASON.

The following are the packs of Hounds hunting in the neighbourhood of the METROPOLITAN RAILWAY, with the Masters, hunting days, and most convenient towns for visitors:—

### STAGHOUNDS.

**Lord Rothschild's.**—LORD ROTHSCHILD—Monday and Thursday. Aylesbury.

**Berkhamsted.**—Mr. J. RAWLE—Wednesday. Berkhamsted, St. Albans and Tring.

(For Berkhamsted book to Chesham Station, thence by road conveyance.)

**Bucks and Berks Farmers'.**—SIR ROBERT WILMOT—Tuesday and Friday. Amersham and Chalfont.

### FOXHOUNDS.

**Berkeley Old (East).**—Mr. R. B. WEBBER—Monday and Thursday, with a bye day. Rickmansworth and Chorley Wood.

**Berkeley Old (West).**—Mr. ROBERT LEADBETTER—Wednesday and Saturday. Amersham, Chalfont and Missenden.

**Bicester and Warden Hill.**—Mr. J. P. HEYWOOD LONSDALE—Monday, Tuesday, Thursday and Saturday. Banbury, Bicester, Brackley, Buckingham *via* Verney Junction and Quainton Road District.

**Whaddon Chase.**—Mr. W. SELBY LOWNDES—Tuesday and Saturday. Aylesbury, Buckingham, Leighton and Winslow Road.

**Grafton.**—Hon. E. S. DOUGLAS-PENNANT—Monday, Wednesday, Friday and Saturday. Buckingham, Brackley, Towcester and Weedon.

The above meets are advertised every Friday, with name of place, in the *Bucks Herald.*

### BEAGLES.

**Berkhamsted** (13½ in. Stud Book Beagles).—Wednesday and Saturday. Mr. W. J. PICKIN. Berkhamsted.

**Bushey Heath** (14 in. pure Beagles).—Saturday, alternate Wednesdays. Mr. R. MAROR. Bushey Heath, Rickmansworth.

**Shardeloes.**—Mr. E. S. S. DRAKE—Shardeloes and Amersham.

**Winslow and District** (Foot Beagles).—Thursdays. Rev. T. SHAKEL.

### DRAGHOUNDS.

**Greenford Drag.**—Mr. PERKINS—Harrow - on - Hill, Greenford District. Saturday.

---

13

# HUNTING

.. IN ..

## BUCKINGHAMSHIRE AND HERTFORDSHIRE.

*For the convenience of HUNTING GENTLEMEN a Train now leaves BAKER STREET at 9.5 a.m. for*

**Rickmansworth arr. 9.50 a.m.**

**Chesham . . . arr. 10.14 a.m.**

**Amersham . . arr. 10.9 a.m.**

**Great Missenden arr. 10.19 a.m.**

**Aylesbury arr. 10.38 a.m.**

*Hunters to be Boxed at Finchley Road by 9.0 a.m.*

### FARES AND RATES.

| | Fares from BAKER ST. | | | | Rates for Hunters from FINCHLEY ROAD. | |
|---|---|---|---|---|---|---|
| | 1st Class. | | 3rd Class. | | | |
| | Single | Return | Single | Return | Single. | Return Same day. |
| RICKMANSWORTH ... | 2/6 | 3/9 | 1/3 | 1/11 | 5/0 | 7/6 |
| CHESHAM ... ... | 3/10 | 5/9 | 1/11 | 2/11 | 7/0 | 10/6 |
| AMERSHAM ... | 3/6 | 5/3 | 1/9 | 2/8 | 6/6 | 9/9 |
| GREAT MISSENDEN ... | 4/4 | 6/6 | 2/2 | 3/4 | 7/9 | 11/8 |
| AYLESBURY ... | 5/10 | 8/9 | 2/11 | 4/5 | 10/0 | 15/0 |

*For Horse Boxes apply to any of the Stations or to the Superintendent of the Line, 32 Westbourne Terrace, W.*

B

Two pages from the Metropolitan Railway Guide of 1904 demonstrate the importance of hunting traffic. Special horse vans were picked up by train at Finchley Road. The goods yard there also handled a considerable traffic in cattle for the London slaughterhouses, as well as dealing with special trains carrying watercress from Chesham and flowers from Uxbridge.

---

the arrival of the Metropolitan Railway in 1892, new housing developments arose around the station, reaching towards Chesham Bois.

After the train left Amersham, an atmosphere of deep rural arcadia soon enclosed the line, with steeply wooded country on the east, the land sloping away towards the classical mansion of Shardeloes on the other side. The great house, which was for many years the home of the Drake family, overlooks a lake formed by the waters of the Misbourne. Fowling was a popular sport here at the turn of the century, and in icy winters people from Amersham would enjoy skating on its frozen surface. Shardeloes possessed one of the largest dovecotes in the county. The railway crossed the main Aylesbury road just north of Little Missenden, one of the tiny jewels of Metro-land. This was the ideal Chilterns village, with two 'pubs', a straggle of cottages and a wonderful old church that suddenly became well known when one of the earliest rediscoveries of medieval wall-paintings was made in the 1930s. 'Hikers' of the age made the place a 'must' for their day. Great Missenden, the next station, has always been an important village. In the early days of the Metropolitan, the train could expect to be met by a string of dog-carts and carriages, conveyances officially recognized by the railway, to whisk away gentlemen to weekend shooting or hunting.

The line continues northwards with grander views, as the Chilterns rise on each side. Away to the east lay other estates — that of the Liberty family at Lee and, beyond, the estates of Lord Rothschild at Tring and at Halton (near Wendover). In 1895 the Metropolitan had built two coaches for the use of Baron Ferdinand de Rothschild and his personal staff. Later the two units were fused into one coach and the 'Rothschild Saloon', as it was then known, continued to be seen at various times on the Metropolitan system as a Directors' coach.

At Wendover the station is well placed at the upper end of the village street. The stop has always been popular, especially for walkers making for the breezy top of nearby Coombe Hill, overlooking the Vale of Aylesbury and the highest point of the Chilterns. Also close to Wendover are the beech-clad slopes dotted with tiny ale-houses that form part of the Chequers estate. Chequers House, on the far side of Coombe Hill, was given to the nation by Lord Lee in 1916 as a country retreat for the Prime Minister of the day. (This station is served today by British Rail trains from Marylebone to Aylesbury, but it still retains its Met footbridges and memories.) The Metropolitan train continued in flat country to Stoke Mandeville (well known today for its hospital for the disabled) and on to Aylesbury, where there is a junction with the lower G.W.R. branch from Princes Risborough, opened in 1863. Aylesbury is the county town of Buckinghamshire and from 1936 until

15

1961 it was the terminus of the passenger services on the Metropolitan line. London Transport services now terminate at Amersham.

One of the most interesting sections of the old Metropolitan Railway was the line beyond to Quainton Road (with the branch to Brill) and Verney Junction. Here, at Verney Junction, the Metropolitan was over fifty miles from Baker Street. The type of traffic carried to the north of Aylesbury was more local and included a high proportion of goods. One of the strongest reasons urged for the expansion of the Metropolitan Railway was to secure its rightful share of the goods traffic originating north of London at a time when the railway's goods receipts came to only 4.5 per cent of the total receipts, other railways' freight receipts accounting for about half. The Metropolitan Railway remained healthy because of dividends from its lands, although the farming country through which the line passed north of Aylesbury did bring in a steady traffic from the carriage of minerals, bricks from Brill and cattle from the Buckingham and Verney estates.

The line from Aylesbury towards Verney Junction, which, as mentioned earlier, started life as a local railway in 1868, was improved for the start of Metropolitan Railway services in the area in 1897. Baron Ferdinand de Rothschild had been building a new classical mansion at Waddesdon and brought pressure to bear on the railway to build a convenient station for his guests, who included Queen Victoria. It had been intended to name the new station 'Lapstones', but this was obviously not going to be good enough for the Baron, and the station opened as Waddesdon Manor in 1897. The 'Lapstone' name was derived from the meadow through which the line ran. On 1 October 1922 the station was renamed Waddesdon. It was reached by a gentle curve from Aylesbury.

Quainton Road, the next stop along the line, was the junction for Brill and is the only station that remains today. It is now the headquarters of the Quainton Railway Society, formed in 1969 to preserve locomotives and rolling stock from a number of lines. Until 1935, the Met's mixed Brill branch train ran from here to the villages of Westcott, Wotton and Brill. The Metropolitan's through services left the Great Central main line at a junction less than half a mile after Quainton Road, curving northwards to climb Hogshaw Bank. The village of Quainton, with its seventeenth-century almshouses and windmill, lies below Quainton Hill, over 600 feet high, to the east of the line. Beyond lay Granborough Road (called Grandborough Road until 6 October 1922). The station had a cattle dock and sidings. From here came a steady traffic of cattle for London, 'two or three trains a week', one old man recalled. Granborough Road and Winslow Road, the final station before Verney Junction, stood amid land owned by Sir Harry Verney. He was the last surviving director of the Metropolitan Railway and was able to tell a shareholders' meeting which voted him on the Board of the railway that he 'owned all the land around two of your stations'.

Verney Junction, where Metropolitan trains joined the Oxford & Cambridge line, was named after an earlier Sir Harry Verney who had with the Duke of Buckingham been responsible for the development of railways in that part of the county. Both Verneys lived to a great age — the Sir Harry after whom the station was named joined in the public luncheon in 1892 to mark the opening of the Metropolitan to Aylesbury. He was then ninety-three. The junior Sir Harry died in 1974 aged ninety-three. Metropolitan trains ran into a bay platform at the junction and until the early 1960s an iron sign on the bridge proclaimed TO THE BOOKING OFFICE & TO THE TRAINS FOR

THE OXFORD & BANBURY BRANCHES & METROPOLITAN LINE. Claydon House, the beautiful home of the Verneys, lies a mile or so away from the station. The house, with its memories of Florence Nightingale and its superb rococo rooms, is now the property of the National Trust.

In Metro-land days, the Brill train steamed out of Quainton Road and round a sharp curve to run parallel to a small lane that eventually joined the main Aylesbury to Bicester road by a level-crossing at Waddesdon Road halt. Here was a small siding for local traffic. The train was usually mixed, for the line ran through farming country, and milk and other farm products were the main source of receipts. Westcott station stood below the hill where Waddesdon Manor was built; the branch line had been used to transport materials for the construction of the mansion. Avoiding high ground, the line ran under the railway spur carrying the Great Central to Grendon Underwood from the Princes Risborough-Birmingham main line. There were two stations at Wotton, and the Metropolitan station had several sidings, the station-master dividing his time between the two stations.

That two railway stations were built within a few yards of each other in a lonely country lane now seems unbelievable. The Great Central spur line had been built in the first place because of the personal wrangles between the Chairman of the Metropolitan, John Bell, and the Great Central Railway's Chairman, William Pollitt. The argument had come to a head when the Great Central's inaugural train, planned to run to Aylesbury and thus over the Great Western line on 30 July 1898, was intercepted at Quainton Road station signal-box by the Metropolitan's Chairman, who had rushed with volunteers from Baker Street as soon as he heard that the new route was being opened up. Claiming that it broke the agreement, Bell personally set a blocking signal against the approaching train and had the satisfaction of seeing it puff to a halt with its train of wagons, then back away ignominiously and disappear northwards again. After this, the Great Central built the Grendon Underwood link north of Quainton Road, beyond the reach of further attack. The new station of course took most of the Metropolitan traffic at Wotton, and trains from Brill carried only a few passengers.

Passing the wooden water tower near Church Siding (a tiny branch ran off to the farm and hamlet of Wotton Underwood) the Brill line curved left and passed over the G.W.R. main line by way of an iron bridge at Wood Siding. Beyond here there was a short spur into the Brill brickworks. Finally, the branch reached the foot of Tram Hill, below the town of Brill. There were a number of sidings and a repair and maintenance shed. This rural retreat was a long way indeed from busy Baker Street, both in distance and atmosphere — the outermost frontier of Metro-land. Here the wind blows fresh and full from the Oxfordshire plains to strike the windmill, Brill's oldest 'inhabitant'. Even today sheep graze the common, and few people are to be found in the main street. Buses are almost unknown to Brill locals drinking noisily in its 'pubs', and sadly, when you ask about the Brill 'Tram' (as it was known), they look sympathetic, as though talking to the mentally handicapped. Brill has forgotten.

### SUBURBIA IN THE MAKING
There were two Metro-lands. The inner part was the Metro-land of Wembley Park, Harrow, Pinner and Ruislip — the land of the new housing estates and the school outings.

Though Middlesex had always felt the influence of

London, in the 1880s the north-west of the county was still an unspoiled landscape of tall elms, massive oak trees, hay fields, winding and often muddy lanes, orchards and hawthorn hedges, brick and timber cottages and old wooden barns with orange tiled roofs. Here, too, were a number of minor country estates: Eastbury at Northwood, Haydon Hall at Eastcote, Swakeleys at Ickenham, Moor Park just over the border in Hertfordshire.

The chief occupation of the Middlesex country folk was the production of hay for the London market. Middlesex was a backward area as far as agriculture was concerned. In fact as early as 1798 John Middleton had written in his *View of the Agriculture of Middlesex* that the outdated farming methods of the 'strong land country westward of Harrow' were held back by 'the deadweight of manorial custom'. Indeed, manorial courts were still held at Ruislip and at Ickenham until the early 1920s. There were few railways except the L.N.W.R. which ran through Harrow and Wealdstone and the G.W.R. branch from West Drayton up to Uxbridge. The only main trunk road was the route through Uxbridge to Oxford.

Carts left for London at 3am from the villages of Ruislip and Pinner. The vehicles were hauled by two horses and also carried a supply of wood faggots which could be thrown into the deeper ruts when the going became rough! It was common for the carts to take over twelve hours for the return trip! None the less the Middlesex countryside had its charms. John Bedford Leno, the Uxbridge Chartist and one-time postman, recorded his travels over the Metroland countryside in the mid-nineteenth century. 'My daily round was through pleasant fields, where birds sang and flowers grew. I saw the squirrel leap from tree to tree, wild rabbits sporting, and the partridge whirring from my feet, the mowers and reapers at their labours, and better still, I was welcomed wherever I went.' And in 1875 the Reverend J.J. Roumieu of Ruislip (then one of the largest parishes in the county) wrote that 'It would seem impossible that such a quiet and secluded spot could exist within 15 miles of Hyde Park Corner; yet when it is remembered that no other place can be found, within this radius, so far from a railway station, our retirement and peace are easily accounted for in our freedom from Sunday excursionists and all similar nuisances.'

Five years later the Metropolitan Railway reached Harrow and, in 1887, Northwood in the north part of Ruislip parish. The 'Sunday excursionists' so deprecated by Roumieu were soon walking and cycling through Ruislip and Pinner.

At Northwood, the local landowner was a gentleman named Carnegie. He realised the potential of the new railway and sold his Eastbury estate to Frank Murray Maxwell Hallowell Carew. Very shortly afterwards Carew was laying out an estate of some 762 acres, with stately and secluded avenues and roads named after his Christian names and those of some of his relations. As well as the large red-brick villas, a few rows of artisan terraces were built down towards the Rickmansworth road. Thus the first Metro-land suburb was born. In 1887 the Metropolitan Surplus Lands Committee was formed; one of its first estates was at Cecil Park, just by Pinner station.

But it was the advent of electrification and the building of the branch to Uxbridge that had such a profound and lasting effect on the Middlesex landscape. Imagine the impact on the villages of Ruislip and Ickenham that the coming of the new railway had! Suddenly, instead of having to drive or walk the miles to Uxbridge Great Western station, you could walk to the Metropolitan station and board a comfortable, well-heated electric train and reach Baker Street some forty minutes later. The

Poster showing just how elaborate the Metropolitan goods services were in 1904. There were no motor lorries to take freight from place to place, and the railway played a vital part in the economy of Metro-land.

Photograph: Authors' Collection

benefits of the twentieth century were suddenly at the cottagers' doorstep. To quote *The Times* on the occasion of the special press trip on the new line made on 13 December 1904: 'Everything which took place conveyed the impression that those present were celebrating the beginning of a new era.'

Indeed, it *was* a new era. Within a few months of the electric trains new houses began to go up at Wembley near the Recreation Park and Great Tower Grounds. There were soon villas amid the shrubberies and green lanes around Pinner and, on a smaller scale, at Ruislip village. It was after the First World War, however, when the Metropolitan Railway Country Estates was formed in 1919 to take over the work of the old Surplus Lands Committee, that the development of the countryside really began. 'Live in Metro-land' became a well-known advertising slogan. It was even engraved on the door plates of the then new Watford compartment stock. The *Metro-land* guide of 1921 stated that: 'The Metropolitan Railway Country Estates have been organized, not merely to provide superior houses in the rural countryside near London, but also to create new Passenger Traffic for the Metropolitan Railway. The Metropolitan Railway Country Estates, therefore, are able to DO more and GIVE more than mere ordinary rent-depending property.'

The Metropolitan Estates Company offered plots of land on which purchasers erected their own houses, which

The Polytechnic Rambling Club on a ramble near Harrow in 1886.
This must be one of the very earliest photographs taken of an organized walking party. At the time most countrymen had to walk everywhere, and only city-dwellers had discovered the urge to get out of town and see the countryside on foot. As suburbia spread, so more people sought the brief hours of fresh air they could enjoy in their six-days-a-week working lives.

All the men and youths (there were no women) are dressed formally and, with the exception of one dissenter, are clad in waistcoats, ties and formal coats. The photograph appears to have been taken during the spring or summer months, yet most members felt the need to carry, and wear, the bowler hats of the time. Almost all sport a watch and chain.

Photograph: Authors' Collection

might be designed either by the Metropolitan's own architect or by a reputable firm. This kind of housing development was really only for the more wealthy, and by the end of the 1920s the Metropolitan was offering estates with ready-built homes. By the end of the Metropolitan Railway's separate existence in 1933, there were houses to suit all incomes in Metro-land. The following selection of estates either developed by the Metropolitan Estates Company or advertised in the *Metro-land* books gives some idea of the extent of housing development between the wars. Some of the claims by the developers make amusing reading and would certainly not have passed today's code of advertising practice (see Alan Jackson's excellent book *Semi-Detached London*).

At Wembley Park the Chalk Hill and Barn Hill estates were built — 'beautiful Barn Hill [was] undoubtedly one of the most attractive estates around London'. Chalk Hill was described as a picturesque and healthy spot; prices began at £1,125. You could also buy a shop with flat above for £2,500 near Wembley Park station. Alas for leafy Chalk Hill! Most of the houses and the very streets were swept away to make way for a gigantic council housing project in the late 1960s.

On the Blackbird Hill estate near the old village of Kingsbury you could buy a plot for £4 10s a foot or a completed house for £750. Semi-detached houses on the Kingsbury Garden Estate cost £725 and were near 'the attractions of Neasden . . . and there are many'. Developments at Queensbury and Canons Park tended to be of terraced housing or small 'sun-trap' style houses. Much of the land around here was built up in the late 1930s.

The Ideal Homes Estate at Stanmore was developed by Henry J. Clare. 'The estate that is different . . . no rows of stereo typed dwellings.' The top-priced houses were as much as £3,500, and there was a special incentive to prospective buyers: 'a saloon car is always at the disposal of intending purchasers.'

In Northwick Park the Woodcock Dell Estate was laid out by the Metropolitan Estates 'on the site of the old Woodcock Dell Farmhouse. Beautiful sites now available at £150.' Nearer Northwick Park station was the Northwick Park Estate. The development was described as

a 'unique specimen of town planning with delightful artistic freehold houses. The Estate includes "The Palaestra" with tennis courts, bowling green and children's playground, tea lounge and a dance room.'

At Rayners Lane was the Metropolitan's Harrow Garden Village Estate built by E.S. Reid. It was advertised over a long period. 'Wherever you choose a house on the estate you may rest assured that you will be surrounded by other E.S. Reid houses . . . you will not have a nasty cheap mass-produced house anywhere near you to lower the value of your property.' Houses began at £895 (bungalows were cheaper). A 'swanky'-looking Tudor-style detached home was yours for £1,250. The houses were grouped around greens and along roads planted with ornamental trees. There were also rows of Tudor-style shops. Along the line in 'the Cityman's ideal suburb' at Eastcote the potential purchaser could 'embrace the opportunity . . . to secure [his] ideal home amid surroundings of unsurpassed natural beauty'. On the Eastcote End Park Estate a residence cost £975! The vast estate built by T.F. Nash at Ruislip Manor developed from about 1932 onwards and was in the form of Tudor-style and 'suntrap' houses in terraces, sometimes in semi-detached pairs. Here the thousands of less-well-paid clerks came and found their homes. By 1939 the area as far south as the Yeading Brook had been covered with street after street.

'At last a wealthy house at low cost . . . £695'. The Bowers estate south of the railway at Ruislip offered 'homes with that cheery touch of brightness that means everything'. Even shades for the electric lights were given away. 'On all sides are green fields and pleasant hedgerows.' Church Croft Estate was east of the High Street and slightly more 'up-market'. Detached houses were £1,000 with space for a garage, or you could buy a plot on the Metropolitan Estate along Eastcote Road and have a house built in your own style. The Swakeleys Estate at Ickenham was developed by Stedman and Clarke throughout the 1920s, but many of the plots did not sell until after the Second World War. Semi-detached houses and bungalows on the Ivy House Farm Estate were advertised at £850.

The Metropolitan's Hillingdon Mount Estate had plots for £4 10s a foot. A space had been reserved for tennis courts. The Hillingdon Estates Company had houses from £725, 'built to sell at a much higher price . . . these houses are filled with all those conveniences so dear to the heart of the housewife and are easy to run as a bijou flat in Town.'

Much of North Harrow was built up by Cutlers Limited. The houses were generally of the mock-Tudor semi-detached type. On the Ridgeway Estate houses were offered at special terms to 'Civil Servants, Bank Officials, Railway and Insurance Officials and L.C.C. Staff Association'. Free travel vouchers were available to view the estate. In Pinner the Cecil Park Estate was the very first Metropolitan development. After the First World War the Grange Estate was advertised with 'exceptionally artistic residences' for £1,600 freehold or (unusually for the Metropolitan Estates) £1,400 leasehold. The Cuckoo Hill Estate was built by W.A. Telling. 'Pinner; the city man's ideal residential suburb . . . villas and spacious plots for sale'. On the Cannoncroft Estate £825 secured the 'ideal bungalow with kitchen cabinet, boiler and an enamelled gas copper'. Payments for this type of home were about 26s 6d a week.

In Northwood the Gatehill and Eastbury Farm Estates were sited on high ground with 'good roads with street lamps'. Northwood was next to that most exclusive suburb, Moor Park, advertised as 'The Gateway to the

Chilterns' and developed by the Unilever Property Department. 'Here one may enjoy quietude and seclusion (without isolation) with all the amenities of residence in an old English Park, yet without the responsibilities of its upkeep'. Fast electric trains took the wealthy stockbrokers to the City in forty minutes.

The Cassiobury Park Estate in Watford was laid out 'in the midst of charming and unspoiled countryside. It comprises the site where stood the Cassiobury Mansion.' Houses started at £1,100 and were built by a number of local firms, including J. Randall. 'Be healthy and happy, come and live at Watford. Homes of distinction for purchasers of discrimination.'

The Metropolitan's Cedars estate covered 600 acres of wooded land in the Chiltern valley between Rickmansworth and Chorley Wood: 'detached residences of the country house type. Artistic design'. Houses began at £975, or you could buy a plot for £600 and consult the Metropolitan's own architect about the design of your home. In Chorley Wood, as well as the Cedars Estate, there was the Chorley Wood Common Estate, with cottage-style homes. Gas and water were laid on but there was no electricity at first.

The Vache estate was nearly two miles from Chalfont station, nearer Chalfont St. Giles in fact. It was built by W.A. Telling of Eastcote with 'select country residences'. Amersham was at the outer limit of estate development. The Weller Estate offered 'a rare opportunity . . . to acquire residences amid the glorious Chilterns, yet only 40 minutes from Town. Semi-detached houses £875.' The 'D' type house at £1,100 was 'specially sited in order to give beautiful views to the Chiltern countryside, the surrounding woods and Old Amersham'. There were also 'semi-bungalows' for as little as £695.

The depression of the 1930s drove many people south to London, among them master builders who found new employment, with some of their craftsmen, in building large areas of housing in Metro-land. The great building boom of prosperous and expanding London was a great contrast with conditions in the rest of the country. Planning permission was easy and the government welcomed the growth because it kept unemployment down and promoted industry. New roads were built, shops, schools, cinemas and factories. Place after place began to grow into townships that were eventually linked up. Buying a house was easy. For example a Rotherham Estate house at Eastcote cost £675 in 1934. You paid £45 down and then about 18s a week for the next twenty years. Some builders even paid moving expenses. Season tickets were cheap, too. A monthly ticket from Eastcote to Liverpool Street was £2 16s, and that was First Class!

A familiar scene on an August walk. The three strong horses wait stolidly, while the horseman tips back his ale. Unlike the London walker, who could hurry away by train, the countryman had no time to spare, and his midday meal was usually taken in the harvest field. Three horse teams were rather unusual, and later models of this reaper were handled comfortably by two animals.

Photograph: County Museum Aylesbury

Moving in was not without its hazards, as a resident of North Harrow wrote in *Excelsior*, a ratepayers' magazine, in 1931. 'I arrived at a station vastly different from the present structure, and stepped into mud of the most adhesive quality I had ever seen or felt! The immediate neighbourhood of the station appeared to be taken up with builders' offices and builders' carts and lorries, and more mud. The winter sunshine glinted on the bright red roofs of little white houses and distant trees, whose bare branches spread like delicate tracery against the clear blue sky.'

These were the years of stained-glass leaded lights in the hall, Austin Seven motor-cars, elaborate picnic baskets, fretwork radio sets, tea parties and bridge evenings and listening to Henry Hall, or spending a Saturday evening at the Odeon. The tradesmen called at the door; travel was swift and cheap and there were special rates to tempt one out into the Chilterns on Sundays. But it was also the end of rural days in Middlesex. Swiftly, so swiftly, the meadows of Kingsbury, Northwood Hills and Rayners Lane became the bright new town. Red London buses appeared; big new multiple shops; flashing neon signs, cinemas and busy highways. It was all new, clean and healthy. 'Residing in suburbia adds a thrill and zest to life. It is a unique experience in having no traditions to live up to,' wrote one of the suburban pioneers in the North Harrow ratepayers' magazine. Traditions were swept away, and many a historic farmhouse and house was demolished. The old landmarks of the day-tripper, The Poplars Restaurant at Ruislip or the ornamental golf club house at Preston Road for instance, went, and so did rural ways such as Rayners Lane. No longer could you start a Metropolitan Railway country walk at, say, Preston Road by following earlier instructions to 'Turn right at the road junction where the sign post points to Clay Lane, then cross into the meadows towards Kenton.'

The Metropolitan Railway had created a new world and a new way of life.

## THE COUNTRY LIFE

Outer Metro-land has always been an essentially rural part of England. Here the beech-clad slopes of the chalk hills merge with the flat, cow-trodden pastures of the Vale of Aylesbury to provide a timeless society that has always been proud of and extremely conscious of English tradition. Its large estates provided some stability in a changing world, yet their owners were also prepared to use the conveniences of the age on their estates and when travelling to London.

Hunting was popular in the early days. Lord

By the 1930s a recognized style of walking dress had evolved, and this party moves purposefully in single file (to tread out the path clearly) down to a typical Chilterns 'Bottom'. Many are ladies prepared to carry their own haversacks, but this was before the days of unisex — most women walkers these days seem to prefer jeans.

Photograph: Authors' Collection

Rothschild's staghounds, and those of the Berkhamsted and Bucks Farmers, provided a meet every weekday between them during the season. And there were foxhounds and beagle packs. Gentlemen could entrain at Baker Street (the horses were loaded at Finchley Road) and join the hunting season out in the country. Later came the cyclist — encouraged out by Metropolitan Railway literature. The Chiltern Hills have always provided splendid walking country. It was the mass weekend visitations of walkers who came by train from London that more than anything else made Metro-land so familiar and so well-loved.

For those who lived in the country and worked on the estates, there was the occasional charitable entertainment laid on by the squire to mark an event, perhaps to honour a visit by the Prince of Wales in the 1890s (for even the Prince was known to have travelled by the Met), or on long-anticipated nights, such as those of Lee Week, part of the summer ritual near Great Missenden, when country-house living was at its height. Lee Manor, near Chesham, home of the Liberty family, was the venue for the endless mixed cricket matches, tennis and dancing parties. The fun always ended with the 'Night Attack' Game. A blast from a hooter at 9.30pm signalled the ascent of a rocket flare, and the 'Missenden Army' of tenants and guests was expected to get through the defences of Lee Manor into the house without being touched. A hearty supper followed. Similar sports events marked the year at Wotton and elsewhere in the county.

Ignoring this jollity, individual craftsmen worked alone in the depths of the beechwoods. These were men called bodgers, a sturdy and independent breed of countrymen who fashioned the raw material from the woods on the spot, with rustic, improvised lathes that used the natural spring of the branches. They are a race of craftsmen that have only recently disappeared.

Few country folk travelled far, except on market day, and fewer still had the price of a fare to spend on the Metropolitan Railway. From the Met & G.C.R. main line at Verney Junction, Pullman expresses hurried business-men to London, but the local trains were only used indifferently. On the Brill branch, a train journey was in any case not easily forgotten! Passengers still recall the 'Tram' with vaguely embarrassed pride. The Brill branch had a colourful past. At first it was worked with horse traction, then after track improvements it seemed to be destined for main-line status as a through Metropolitan line to Oxford. After the line was leased to the Metropolitan, it kept its wayward life, for only on very rare occasions would a through train be run. Here was country life at its topsy-turvy best — an ancient locomotive that once ran on the old steam Inner Circle in London and an antique train! Speed was low, yet even so a lady's maid at Wotton Underwood managed to get herself run over — an event never really explained and, with such a slow, steamy

The Chiltern bodger was a craftsman who worked usually alone, deep in the heart of his raw material — the beechwoods. At the entrance to his improvised hut, which he had roughly thatched and protected from the hill breezes by wood shavings, he is finishing a chair leg with his spokeshave, judging his work with careful, practised eye. These fine old rural characters have been found dead at their work, for they seldom retired. Even after the Second World War there were still some bodgers at work in the Chilterns, and the local towns of High Wycombe and Chesham gained a reputation for wood-turning and chair-making, inheriting the old tradition.

Photograph: County Museum Aylesbury

death-blow, carrying the undertones of suicide.

The trains continued to leave the track occasionally! Nobody really worried. One lady recalls how the driver collected a team of nineteen labourers and vagrants from the nearby fields to help to lift the carriage back on to the line, after which the train proceeded to Brill. Another person remembers that, in the early 1930s, the train stopped half a mile from Brill. After a long wait, she noticed the engine faraway. Her shouting attracted the attentions of the stationmaster-cum-porter who explained, 'We just forgot we had a passenger.'

The village community at Wotton Underwood, to which wagons were occasionally shunted to Church Siding, was complete with church, large house, farm, cottages and school. It is still the same today.

The Brill branch train fitted easily into the local picture, the older children using the train for schooling further away. The train would be held for the regulars. On one occasion a schoolgirl arrived too late even for this understanding arrangement. The train had gone. The stationmaster at Wotton, however, was aware of Met tradition. Shouting, he managed to gain the attention of the driver as the train was remorselessly disappearing through the fields and it shunted back to allow the young lady to take her seat.

The service to Verney Junction and Brill failed to survive for long after the Metropolitan Railway died in 1933. The Brill line was closed in 1935, and passenger services to Verney Junction ceased on 4 July 1936, although a Great Central special was run along the line on the following day.

# THE EARLY YEARS

## BAKER STREET TO STANMORE

# CHILTERN COURT, THE GATEWAY TO METRO-LAND

The first Baker Street station dated from 1863. The St. John's Wood Railway platforms were built in 1868, but when the line was extended to Harrow and beyond they soon became inadequate. By 1903 Baker Street station was handling 929 trains a day. In 1912 a long-overdue rebuilding scheme began. A hotel was planned to complement the new station — and the Metropolitan's main-line image. But the First World War intervened, and afterwards it was decided to build a block of luxury flats. So Chiltern Court was born. The designer was the Metropolitan's own architect, C.W. Clark.

Between 1927 and 1929 one of the tallest cranes ever seen in London at that time worked away on the project. The completed building contained 180 suites, ranging from ten to three rooms in size. Annual rent was from £300 and each flat had a relay radio and a Hobbe-Hart jewel safe 'in an unobtrusive position'. The famous came to live there, including H.G. Wells and Arnold Bennett, who died in his flat in 1931. The building included the Chiltern Court Restaurant. Beneath its ceiling, decorated with the arms of the various places reached by the Metropolitan, 250 people could dine, with an orchestra playing from a balcony.

Photograph: Authors' Collection

## METRO LUXURY

Taking it easy after a hard day in the City, businessmen relax in one of the Met's two Pullman cars at Baker Street one day in the 1930s. The Metropolitan Pullman services began on 1 June 1910 and ran until 7 October 1939. They provided comforts undreamt of by today's commuters: arm-chairs, carpets and a bar, plus light refreshments. For a 6*d* supplement (1*s* after Rickmansworth) to the First-Class fare you could travel home with your workday nerves soothed by a 'gin and splash'. There were also two late evening runs: the 10.06pm to Chorley Wood and the midnight 'theatre' run out to Aylesbury and Verney.

Interior view of one of the Pullman cars. 'Pullman cars are run daily (except Sundays) between London and Aylesbury, stopping at such golf courses as Northwood, Moor Park . . . and providing communi-cation with a number of delightful places along the edge of the Chilterns. . .' *(The Golden Way* Pullman Guide 1935).

Photograph: London Transport

## PASSING WEST HAMPSTEAD

Metropolitan-Vickers electric locomotive 'Sir Christopher Wren' and down Pullman train in about 1928. There were twenty electric locomotives, built in 1922 and all named after people or places connected with Metro-land. The first West Hampstead station was demolished to make way for the Great Central Railway; the platform in this picture dates from 1897/8 and was replaced in 1938 by a single island platform.

Photograph: Authors' Collection

## RURAL NEASDEN

Fields and trees and a winding lane to the 'Spotted Dog' — a rural Neasden of 1896 that is now long forgotten. Today it is all roaring traffic, supermarkets and cafes, and rows of terraced houses dating from the 1920s and 1930s.

This train is just pulling out of the original 'Kingsbury' station, with Beyer Peacock locomotive 'Dido' of 1864 and a set of 8-wheel and 4-wheel carriages. Quite a crowd has left the train — some of the early Metro-land commuters. 'Dido' was sold to the South Hetton Coal Co. in 1905 and subsequently rebuilt as a 6-coupled engine in 1910.

Photograph: London Borough of Brent

## END OF THE ROAD

Some of the Beyer Peacock locomotives being broken up at Neasden in about 1906, after electrification had made them redundant. According to the records, a number of the engines were sold to Fraser and Co. for scrap. In the background is the chimney of the coal gas plant that supplied fuel for the carriage lighting in steam days. The gas was compressed and carried in cylinders in the carriage roof.

The Metropolitan had laid out the works at Neasden in 1888, replacing the old cramped locomotive works at Edgware Road. A small village was built to house the workers, streets and flats being named after the more distant parts of the Metropolitan system (Quainton Street, Verney Street etc).

Photograph: H.C. Casserley Collection

## DEATH OF A GODDESS

Last days of 'Juno', Beyer Peacock Number 3 at Neasden, 1907. She is awaiting her fate with another engine of the same class.

Photograph: Sigrist Collection

## COLLISION COURSE

Despite heavy traffic, the Metropolitan suffered few accidents. One exception was on the foggy morning of 26 October 1907, when, standing at West Hampstead, the 7.37am to Willesdon Green was run into by the next down train. Three people lost their lives. The damaged trains were towed back to Neasden and part of the wreckage is seen here being examined by some of the more important Metropolitan staff. One of these cars, Number 46, was converted into a gauging car to test the route for the introduction of the Pullman cars in 1910.

Photograph: Sigrist Collection

## END OF THE 8-WHEELERS

Set of the old and uncomfortable Second- and Third-Class 8-wheeled stock of *c.*1867 in the hands of the breakers at Neasden in 1907 after electrification. To the left is the power station, which was built for the electrification of 1904/5. It was subsequently extended to provide extra electric power in 1908, 1910, 1921 and 1922.

Photograph: Authors' Collection

## WELCOME FOR A NEW ARRIVAL

The year 1907 seems to have been an eventful one for the photographer at Neasden. In addition to a collision and the breaking-up of old steam stock, there was also the arrival of the British Thomson Houston electric locomotive, which with the slightly earlier British Westinghouse machines formed the original fleet of electric locomotives. The body on the engine shown here was built by the Metropolitan Amalgamated Railway Carriage and Wagon Co.

The three chimneys on the building behind were the outlets for the gas-making plant. The gas was used to illuminate the steam carriages, and at times the smell over this part of the works was overpowering. The signal is a hand-controlled stop; a portion of the blade extends beyond the spectacles so as to minimize the effect of snow building up on the arm and lowering it into the 'off' position.

Photograph: Sigrist Collection

**NEASDEN SPORTS, 1909**

It wasn't all work on the old Met. Here is R. Whitley winning the annual one-mile handicap at the 1909 Railway sports day. This picture really captures the spirit of the patriotic late Edwardian period: the Union Jack flying by the finishing-line, the straw boaters (or 'yards') and the demure glance from a pretty miss at the only pair of knees in sight!

Photograph: Sigrist Collection

GENERAL VIEW OF WEMBLEY PARK. AS SEEN FROM RAILWAY STATION, SHEWING TOWER AS IT WILL APPEAR WHEN COMPLETE, TOTAL HEIGHT 1150 FEET.

SKETCH PLAN SHEWING PROXIMITY OF PARK TO STATION. FROM BAKER ST

## WATKIN'S FOLLY

In 1889 Sir Edward Watkin, Chairman of the Metropolitan, visited Paris and was so impressed with the popularity of the newly-built Eiffel Tower that he decided to construct a similar one in London. The Eiffel Tower's takings were £1,800 a day, construction costs had been repaid in seven months, and Watkin thought that his tower would bring additional profits to the Met. A number of sites presented themselves, including the triangle of land near Gloucester Road and High Street Kensington stations. Eventually 280 acres at Wembley Park were bought. Gladstone asked questions in the House on Watkin's behalf, and a committee reported patriotically that 'although the atmosphere of London may not be so favourable to extensive views as Paris, the view would be incomparably superior.'

In 1890 a Metropolitan Tower Company was formed and a competition announced for the design. The winner was to receive 500 guineas. There were many weird and fantastic entries. The final design was by Stewart McLaren and Dunn, and shortly afterwards the International Tower Company was formed to finance the actual construction. But there was only lukewarm response from the investing public. The tower only reached 150 feet — and then the money ran out.

The partly completed tower opened on 18 May 1896 and this optimistic poster appeared to tempt the crowds out into the country to see such attractions (apart from the views) as Buffalo Bill's Wild West Show and fireworks' displays. At the bottom right-hand corner of the poster there is a plan of the original Wembley Park station.

Photograph: London Borough of Brent

29

## DOWN SHE GOES!

Watkin's Wembley Tower had little effect on the profits of the Metropolitan. It did have unfortunate long-term repercussions though. The Great Central Railway was then planning its Marylebone extension and had long sought to rid itself of the irksome agreement with the Metropolitan concerning running powers into London. The Great Central suggested that the 'success' of the Tower meant that there would be insufficient capacity on the Metropolitan tracks to accommodate the main-line trains because of the crowds going to Wembley.

John Bell, the Chairman of the Metropolitan, knew by early 1895, when the suggestion was made, that the Tower scheme was a hopeless failure, yet he was unwilling (or unable) to be frank enough to convince the Great Central that this was so. The Great Central had laid its plans for an independent line and was in no mood to listen. The Tower's failure also had a decisive influence on Watkin's scheme for a trunk line to the Channel, as public confidence was sapped.

This dramatic and hitherto unpublished picture was taken on 9 September 1907. It shows the Tower meeting its end by explosive charges before being cut up and sold for scrap abroad. The blast from the explosion that has just tumbled one of the great supporting legs can be seen clearly, as well as the staging level, which lies on the ground beyond. The massive concrete foundations were not finally removed until the construction of Wembley Stadium in 1922.

Photograph: Sigrist Collection

## WONDERFUL WEMBLEY—1

'Let us go to Wembley where may be seen such wonders as have never before been gathered together in one place of the world' (guide to the British Empire Exhibition, 1924).

The British Empire Exhibition was a result of a proposal made before 1914 by Lord Strathcona. The government guaranteed £100,000, provided that a further sum of £500,000 was subscribed. The Metropolitan Railway itself guaranteed up to £20,000.

The appearance of rural Wembley Park was completely changed as the Exhibition buildings went up. This picture from 1921 shows the start of the work. At the top right are the foundations of the Stadium; above the Metropolitan station (bottom) and the trees are the remains of the Wembley Park golf course, with the sites of the pavilions being laid out.

The newly-built Metropolitan station, which replaced the old two-platformed station of 1894, was described as 'one of the finest and most efficiently equipped stations erected for handling large crowds'. It was used by 11,500,00 people in 1924 (at one time during the Exhibition 1,000 people a minute were passing through the barriers). A service of 650 trains a day was provided.

The bottom right of the picture shows the goods yard. At one time a long siding from here led into the park and was used to carry materials for the Tower. The track was used later for experiments with electric traction. Today the remains of the exhibition are a sad sight.                    Photographs: Aerofilms Limited

## WONDERFUL WEMBLEY—2

Cover of the special edition of *Metro-land* for 1924. The great Palace of Engineering remains but is now open to the sky, and the other buildings that are left are factories and warehouses. But the vast Stadium lives — a monument to the Exhibition and a memorial to the Tower, for the site of that folly is now the centre of the famous Wembley pitch!

Photograph: Authors' Collection

## TRAIN CREW, 1931

Wembley Park has always been a changeover point for train crews. Here the motorman sits between two guards. The uniform of the guards confirms the importance of their job. Gold braiding decorates the peak of their wired hats, and each man carries his regulation whistle attached by a chain. The lapels of the uniform carried the words 'Metropolitan Railway' worked in gold wire. The man on the right is the father of one of the authors of this book.

Photograph: Authors' Collection

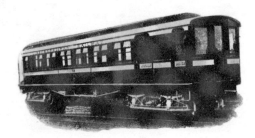

## STANMORE . . . 'THE NEW ADDITION TO METRO-LAND'

The branch to Stanmore opened up a large tract of unspoiled countryside for housing development. The Development Act which permitted construction received Royal Assent on 4 June 1930, having been welcomed by the government as a means of relieving unemployment. Construction involved diverting the Wealdstone Brook and digging cuttings from Canons Park to Stanmore.

This train of contractor's wagons filled with very heavy, very wet Middlesex clay was somewhere at the southern end of the line in the wet summer of 1931. The locomotive is one of the Manning Wardle 0-6-0 saddle tanks used by the contractors, Walter, Scott and Middleton Limited. Her name is 'Alexandra', and she was built in 1901.

Photograph: Authors' Collection

## THE SPECIAL OPENING TRAIN

A comparatively rare photograph of the official opening train passing through the Kingsbury cutting on 9 December 1932. The train was a unique combination of 'T' compartment stock, one of the Pullman cars and the Rothschild Saloon. The electrical arrangements must have caused some headaches at Neasden! The branch was opened by the Minister of Transport, P.J. Pybus, and the public service began the next day with a schedule of 144 trains a day, although many of these were worked only as far as Wembley Park. The Stanmore terminus and the station buildings at Kingsbury were in C.W. Clark's 'Metro. Suburban Villa' style.

Photograph: *Railway Magazine*

## BRAVE NEW KINGSBURY

'Large tracts of land have already been secured by enterprising builders along the route, to be in readiness for development when the line is opened' (advertisement in *Metro-land*, spring 1932).

How rapidly development took place. The picture of the official opening train shows that there were already houses along the line. This photograph of Kingsbury station dates from a short time after the line opened. Semi-detached houses are being completed in the background, and the house immediately to the right of the station is the show office for Prince and Co. the estate developers.

Photograph: London Borough of Brent

## STANMORE TO BAKER STREET

One of the original 'MU' stock electric motor cars and train leaving Wembley Park in 1933. the 'MU' stock was one of the most powerful electric multiple unit trains in the world when it was introduced on the Watford service in 1926. The 'MU' cars can be distinguished from the later 'MV' compartment stock by the negative shoe fuse (seen to the left of the couplings) and the buffers and vacuum brake pipe. On the far left of the picture is the old Wembley Park Platform 6, now demolished.

Photograph: London Transport

# OUT FROM LONDON

## PRESTON ROAD TO HARROW-ON-THE-HILL

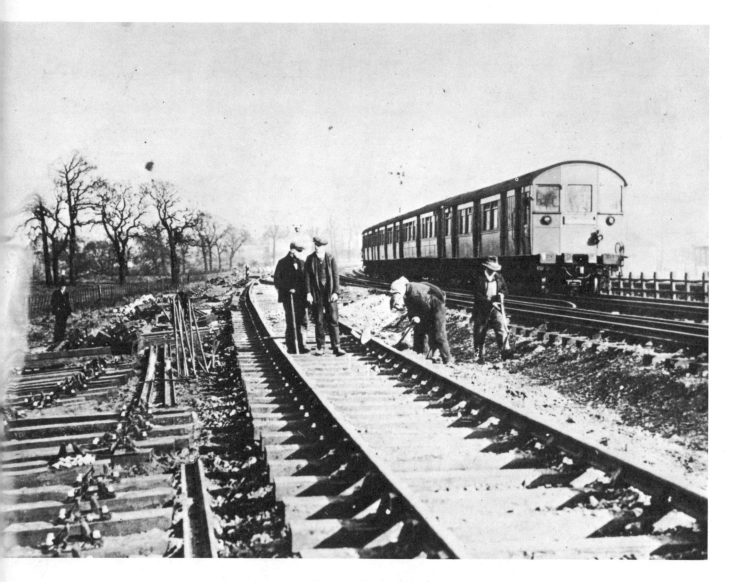

## WIDENING THE LINE

The 1930 Development Act allowed the Metropolitan not only to build the Stanmore branch but also to quadruple the line between Wembley Park and Harrow. The track quadrupling was carried out, under the supervision of G.A. Wilson, Chief Engineer, along the 'up' side and involved the construction of embankments, as well as concrete retaining walls at Northwick Park. New stations at Preston Road and Northwick Park were built by the Pitcher Construction Co. The widening project was completed on 22 November 1931. This photograph shows track laying under way on the Wembley Park side of Preston Road. The train of saloon stock is bound for Uxbridge.

Photograph: Authors' Collection

## RURAL PRESTON 1920

From Wembley rise and Kenton stream,
From Preston Farm and hollow,
Where Lyon dreamed, and saw in dream,
His race of sons to follow.

So runs a verse in an old guidebook. This was the country of Lyon, the founder of Harrow School in Elizabethan times. Even in 1919 it was still a remote district. 'The prospects of Preston Road still remain in the future. It is pure country around here, with a house or two scattered here and there over the landscape.' Photograph: Authors' Collection

The original Preston Road halt (on the Wembley side of the road bridge), opened in May 1908 for the Olympic Games Clay Pigeon Shoot at the Uxendon Shooting School nearby. Photograph: Authors' Collection

## HARROW GOLF CLUB

'To the City man the "Met" is a short cut to the nearest golf course. From his office he can step in at any of the "Met" stations close by and be taken in a few minutes by electric train, to the links without change' (*Metro-land,* early 1920s).

This view of the ornate club house was taken from the road bridge by the old station, probably at the time of the last season in about 1930. Certainly by 1931 the last fields on the slopes of Woodcock Hill were being laid out for building, and the golf course was soon covered in streets and houses.

Photograph: London Borough of Brent

## RACING TO HARROW

Metropolitan-Vickers electric locomotive and Pullman train, with L.N.E.R. express racing towards Harrow near Northwick Park. The Metropolitan locomotive is Number 18 'Michael Faraday' and the train is made up of 'Dreadnought' stock. 'Michael Faraday' was withdrawn on 7 March 1962.

Photograph: London Transport

## CLASSIC STEAM

Beyer Peacock locomotive number 3 'Juno' with train of assorted 8- and 4-wheelers. It has just passed under the old Sheepcote Lane (now Watford Road) bridge *en route* to Harrow in the 1890s. The Great Central Railway is under construction on the right.

Photograph: H.C. Casserley Collection

## EARLY ELECTRIC

One of the original British Westinghouse 'camel-back'- or 'steeple'-type electric locomotives heads one of the first Pullman trains to Baker Street in 1910. The carriages are some of the 'Bogie' stock type built by the Ashbury Carriage and Iron Company between 1898 and 1900. From the later part of 1910 the Pullman cars ran with the new 'Dreadnought' carriages.

Photograph: Authors' Collection

## 'CAMEL-BACK' AT HARROW

The first of the ten British Westinghouse electric locomotives was delivered in April 1905. The locomotives originally carried very large and ugly destination blinds on their fronts, but by the time this picture was taken in about 1921 they had been replaced by metal plates. The trains ran beyond Baker Street direct to Liverpool Street, linking with the Great Eastern. The schoolboy watching is from one of the many private schools in Harrow.

Photograph: London Transport

## HOME FROM SCHOOL

School's out and it's home to tea with mother: a little girl sits on the seat waiting for the Uxbridge branch train in 1933. Harrow attracted a number of private schools and the Metropolitan carried large numbers of pupils every day from establishments such as the Lower School of John Lyon, Bowden House, Orley Farm, Heathfield, St Margaret's and the Boys' High School.

The advertisements on the station are interesting. Constance Bennett is appearing in *Sealed Lips* at the Embassy Cinema, North Harrow, and you could 'Buy your House through the Hearts of Oak Building Society' or get the *Star* and read about the latest exploits of Jack Hobbs.

Photograph: London Transport

## HARROW STATION

When the original station, built in a 'modified Queen Anne' style, was opened on 2 August 1880, there was great rejoicing in Harrow. Now there was a train service to London every ten minutes instead of the slow and infrequent services offered by the L.N.W.R. at Wealdstone.

The entrance to the station, shown here, was originally on the 'Hill' side, but with the growth of the town area of Greenhill on the north side the emphasis changed to the other entrance in College Road, and the station itself was rebuilt in 1938.

Photograph: London Borough of Harrow

## HARROW FROM THE AIR

Only an aerial picture can show what an area was really like in the past. This is the district around the Metropolitan station at Harrow in 1921. A train of saloon stock is leaving for Baker Street (bottom right corner), and the open-top bus (bottom left) is probably on London General route 18. The tennis courts, buildings and circular path round the park are on the site of Lowlands, once the estate of Benjamin Rotch, Deputy Lord Lieutenant of Middlesex. The houses on the right of the picture along College Road have all gone except for the tallest building with the small square of open land at the back (Heathfield school). Top left of the station is the Metropolitan Railway's electric sub-station of 1905, the only part of the old station now left.

Photographs: Aerofilms Limited

## OFF TO THE COUNTRY

Funereal from Harrow draws the train,
On, on, north westwards, London far away,
And stations start to look quite countrified.
(Sir John Betjeman)

An Aylesbury-bound train pulls out of Harrow in 1920/1 with an 'H' class locomotive (designed by Charles Jones). The train is composed of some interesting stock: a milk van (one is preserved at the London Transport Collection); 1910 'Dreadnought' carriages and a Bogie carriage. The signal box was the original 'Harrow Station' box and was demolished in 1948.

Photograph: H.C. Casserley Collection

# THE UXBRIDGE BRANCH

## WEST HARROW TO UXBRIDGE

## WEST HARROW IN THE RAIN

Fast electric trains to London! Suburban development at West Harrow started very early; the station
was opened in 1913 and houses followed shortly
afterwards. West Harrow was an extension of Harrow

itself and as such not really Metro-land. The streets
were named after famous headmasters of the School:
Drury, Vaughan and Butler. The train up on the
bridge is one of the 'MW' compartment stock trains
(later known as the 'T' stock).

Photograph: London Transport

## THE ORIGINAL WOODEN HALT

Narrow, twisting Rayners Lane ran from Roxeth
(South Harrow) to Marsh Lane, Pinner, and took its
name from Daniel Rayner, a farmer who had lived in
a small farmstead on the way to Pinner in Victorian
days. The old house, stock and lands were put up for
auction on 30 August 1928, and the land was
purchased by the Metropolitan Railway Country
Estates. The station, which was opened on 25 May
1906, was in a lonely spot — 'two or three well
separated houses, a sewage farm and a rifle range'.
District Railway services to South Harrow started on
28 June 1903, but although the Metropolitan built a
connecting line over a viaduct from Rayners Lane it
was only used by coal traffic for Roxeth Gas Works
until the District trains began running through to
Uxbridge on 1 March 1910.

Rayners Lane was still remote in the late 1920s. At
Christmas 1927 the line was blocked with snow drifts
and passengers were stranded for four and a half
hours, huddled in the tiny waiting huts seen in this
photograph, which dates from 1933. The workmen
here seem to be making running repairs! The Robinson
estate in High Worple and Worple Way was the first
development at Rayners Lane (1929/32). 'The estate
is carefully laid out with due regard to artistic arrangement' (*Metro-land,* 1930s).

In the early 1930s about 22,000 people used the
station every year. By 1939 the figure was four
million! Few other places around London had grown
so rapidly over so wide an area. The present station
was opened on 30 August 1938.

Photograph: London Transport

## RURAL RAYNERS LANE

A view along the Lane to Pinner in about 1930. The young lady is the daughter of the editor of *Metro-land*.

Photograph: Authors' Collection

## URBAN RAYNERS LANE

Very soon the Metropolitan Railway Country Estates began to lay out the Harrow Garden Village estate here, with chalets, houses and bungalows grouped around village greens or along avenues planted with flowering trees. Rows of neo-Tudor shops were built, while south of the station T.F. Nash began the vast housing estate of terraced and semi-detached 'Tudor' houses, with stained-glass front doors and pebble-dash-finish walls. The developers were so proud of their estate ('no stereo-typed layouts') that a gala opening week was held and a triumphal arch erected over the new shopping street, with a grand fireworks' display.

Photograph: Authors' Collection

## EARLY EASTCOTE

The 1924 edition of *Metro-land* described Eastcote as 'one of the most charming villages in Middlesex. The real charm of the place consists of the old farmhouses, with their red-tiled barns, a few half-timbered dwellings and a number of picturesque cottages, with gardens where flowers grow in gay profusion.' This picture shows the halt soon after it opened in 1906, with a train hauled by a B.T.H. unit approaching from Rayners Lane.

One of the first season-ticket holders at Eastcote was Mr G.A. Joce — a yearly Second-Class season to Baker Street cost £8 10s then. He recorded that: 'There was no booking office at first — tickets were bought on the train. Trains stopped on notice to the guard. I was often the only passenger alighting at 6pm.' W.A.G. Kemp, a local historian, remembered going along Field End Road to the station one night in the 1920s: 'How dark the road was; quite uncanny; no traffic, no sign of life, no light, except from the moon and stars.'

Photograph: Authors' Collection

**SUBURBIA IN THE MAKING**
Eastcote station in the early 1930s. The old booking hut and kiosk shops stood beside what had been a rough roadway, and beyond the bridge are just visible the first of the new shops under construction — plus lots of mud and builder's rubble.

Photograph: London Borough of Hillingdon

## A DAY IN THE COUNTRY

The dusty streets and noisy trams of Willesden Green and Kilburn High Road have been left behind; eager young faces, noses pressed to the glass of the compartment windows, look for the first glimpse of Harrow Hill as the train leaves Wembley Park; the excitement grows as the old carriages rattle down the fly-under after Harrow and pass through West Harrow and Rayners Lane. Here is the real country at last. Elms and oaks, cows and sheep. Carrier bags bulging with sandwiches, fruit cake and lemonade bottles. The train comes to a halt at Eastcote and the teachers and helpers guide the rush of shouting, merry children up the slope and into narrow Field End Road. For many children this is their first trip to the country. Doors slam; children shout; a happy day lies ahead at The Pavilion pleasure grounds.

In this picture a train of 'Bogie' stock (converted from steam carriages for multiple electric working) unloads. The covered 'up' platform behind the train was provided to shelter the ever-increasing excursion traffic when the weather proved wet.

Photograph: Authors' Collection

## THE PAVILION

Year after year, the Sunday School and club trains brought London's children (and also the adults) for a day at The Pavilion, which stood along Field End Road. The Pavilion pleasure grounds were owned by Captain Albert Bayly of the Salvation Army. 'Well over a million and a half kiddies and grown-ups . . . have spent the day of their lives during the past 30 years at The Pavilion,' claimed a 1931 advertisement. There were thirty-two acres of sports fields, with roundabouts, swings and donkeys. If it did rain (but did it ever?) accommodation for 4,000 people under cover was available. This picture shows a few lining up for The Pavilion's 'Grand National'!

Photograph: Authors' Collection

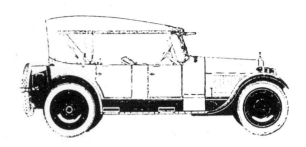

## THE DANSANT

Forget the threat of the dole queue; forget the depression; never mind the man with the little moustache who seems to be causing a nuisance in Germany. Eat your watercress sandwiches and scones — there's plenty of butter; take a stroll through the Eastcote meadows or dance to the sound of Howard Godfrey's Warldorfians and Al Bowley crooning 'Fancy our meeting'. But hurry, hurry, the march of progress is underway, and where you dance and wander will soon be rows of semi-detached houses, tiny lawns and rose trees.

The Pavilion was sold in 1935, and so ended the tourist era in Middlesex.

Photograph: Authors' Collection

50

## BIRTH OF A SUBURB

This scene at Ruislip Manor in 1932 is typical of the state of many suburban roads when rain came. The halt was originally opened in 1912 to serve the eastern end of the projected Ruislip Garden City, but its sole stationman had to join up in the First World War, so the station was closed for long periods. The plan was based on contemporary ideas of Garden Cities such as Letchworth and Welwyn. There was to be a grand avenue from Ruislip Woods in the north to Ruislip Junction (South Ruislip) in the south, with a series of intersecting and impressive squares around which the principal houses and shops would be grouped. Ruislip-Northwood Urban District Council was the first local authority to produce a town plan (1908), but only a dozen or so of the houses were ever built. After the 1914-18 conflict, different and less ambitious ideals prevailed. Just under the bridge workmen are building the estate office for the vast T.F. Nash estate.

Photograph: London Borough of Hillingdon

## GROWTH OF A SUBURB

The same car (the architect's?) and the completed estate office show that work has progressed. The concrete roadway is the start of the 'grand avenue' which was to become Victoria Road. The sign-writer is about to start painting a notice — perhaps 'T.F. Nash Limited. Houses 12/3 per week £450 freehold'. Just behind the estate office are rows of sign-boards that will be put up as each house is sold. In the background are some of the houses on the Bowers Estate at Shenley Avenue, Ruislip.

Photograph: London Borough of Hillingdon

## 'AIN'T SHE BEAUTIFUL TO SEE?'

That might have been the comment of the gent standing on the platform on the left as the official opening the train on the Harrow Uxbridge Railway drew into Ruislip on 30 June 1904. The decorated locomotive is Metropolitan 'E' class Number 1 (the original Number 1 had been scrapped). She was built at Neasden and travelled many thousands of miles over the Metropolitan system, living on into the 1950s as L44. Now she is being restored to her original appearance at the Quainton Railway Centre. The rolling stock of the train is made up of 8-wheelers, Numbers 41 and 45 (with original straight top doors) and the Rothschild Saloons, plus brake 3rd carriages. This particular formation was kept for special hire work and for the use of Baron Ferdinand de Rothschild of Halton House near Wendover.

The Rothschild Saloons, made for the Baron to use on his frequent visits to London, were built by Brown, Marshalls & Company; each saloon cost £660 in 1895. The carriages had similar layouts and the furnishings of the carriages were like the Victorian family saloons used by many railways at this period. A year after this picture was taken, the saloons were sent to Neasden and rebuilt as a single 58 feet-long vehicle, with interior furnishings by Maples. This carriage was then sometimes used as a standby for one of the Pullman cars and as a Directors' coach.

Photograph: London Transport

## HAYMAKING NEAR RUISLIP

A traveller in the opening train on the Uxbridge line wrote: 'Here were stretches of meadowland with herds of sleek cattle grazing lazily, there the chink and rattle of the grass cutting machines. Again, to mark, as it were, the rural aspect of the new line, plump partridges raised their startled heads, and a pheasant, with all its glorious plumage shining like burnished gold, ran to cover. All this almost within sound of Bow Bells, Ruislip in all its rural beauty was soon reached.'

Photograph: County Museum Aylesbury

## RUISLIP VILLAGE

A long main street leads to the old village centre by St Martin's church and Manor Farm, all around are fields and woods. The Met station and its approach road are in the bottom left corner. There is already — for this is 1921 — some housing development on the left of the picture, in King's End and King Edward's Road. The short section of roadway just above the station by the parade of shops later became busy Pembroke Road. The winding, rural lane above is Brickwall Lane, which led to the halt at Ruislip Manor. In the large field above the lane the Catholic Church is under construction; the foundation stone had been laid only a month or so before this picture was taken. By the end of the 1930s land values had risen so much that the building was demolished and replaced by shops. The large open field was developed as The Croft Estate — 'houses with the dignity and distinction so much sought after by gentlefolk'. The site of the farmhouse and rickyard on the left of the High Street in the centre of the picture is now occupied by the local branch of Woolworth, while in the trees beyond at the junction of Ickenham Road and High Street stood 'The Poplars', the much-loved tea gardens and centre for school outings.

Photographs: Aerofilms Limited

## THE POPLARS

The Poplars was famous from the early days of Metro-land. There you could get a lunch of roast beef, York ham or pork, fruit tarts and coffee all for 1s 6d or afternoon tea (with three kinds of cake, buttered scones and jam or watercress) for 9d. The thirsty cyclist could cool down with a bottle of R. White's lemonade for 2d, while the more affluent visitor might stay overnight for a few shillings. 'The Poplars' became famous because of a music-hall song written about it:

'Neath the shade of the Ruislip 'Poplars'
    We go by cycle for a country trip,
    Every man in London will tell you,
    About the merry Poplars at Ruislip.

And they spend the day with Rose you see,
    At 'The Poplars' where sweet Bluebell serves tea,
    And Lily's white hands bring cakes and jam,
    And don't we enjoy Miss Pansy's cold lamb.

The jellies and custards by Poppy and May,
    And the cream brought by Daisy is as sweet as hay,
    It's a very short distance by rail on the 'Met',
    And at the gate you'll find waiting Sweet Violet.

This picture shows some of the girls and the visitors outside the old house some time before the First World War. The Poplars was owned by George Weedon, a wealthy local man, and for the 1913 season the girls were dressed in green and white outfits, with white shoes and caps. Each waitress also wore an imitation flower of her 'name'.

Photograph: London Borough of Hillingdon

## A RIVAL FOR CUSTOM

There were rival establishments, of course. Along the road to
Ickenham by Sharps Lane was The Orchard-Bungalow, owned by Mr
D.P. Wood. This group posed for the photographer on a summer day
when Edward VII was still King. Perhaps school parties eventually
proved too boisterous for Mr Wood because at a later date he was
advertising 'Parties catered for, except school treats. It's really in an
orchard.' The building was enlarged between the wars and became the
Orchard Hotel Restaurant.

Photograph: London Borough of Hillingdon

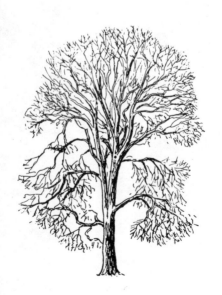

## ICKENHAM HALT

'What, a halt out in the wilds of Ickenham!' was the comment of an Uxbridge councillor when the residents of Ickenham asked for a halt to be opened on the Harrow & Uxbridge Railway. But they got their halt — on 25 September 1905. Unfortunately, the platforms were only capable of handling three-car trains, so that longer trains had to pull up twice. The platforms were lengthened in July 1922.

A booking hut was opened in 1910 (you can see it up on the bridge with the newsagent's kiosk on its left and the electric sub-station beyond). In order to attract passengers, the Metropolitan flew a large red flag. Unfortunately, it flapped so wildly in the wind one January day that a horse being led along Glebe Lane bolted, injuring the man with it. A court case ensued and the Metropolitan was fined and ordered to remove the flag.

When the housing estates were being built, the local roads were so muddy in winter that residents walked to the station in Wellington boots. The stationman labelled them and stored them in the hut, while their owners put on their everyday shoes for the journey to London.

Photograph: London Borough of Hillingdon

## THE VILLAGE CENTRE

The Edwardian visitor to Ickenham could refresh himself in Glebe Lane near the station at Cowne's Orchard (accommodation for 200) or he could go along a few hundred yards to the village centre, with its pond and pump and call at Miss Butler's Post Office and store (just to the left of the little girl in the centre of this picture). Miss Butler ran the shop until 1939, by which time suburban parades of modern shops had been built and the local lanes had become busy dual-carriageways.

The ivy-clad 'Coach and Horses' in the centre of this view offered overnight accommodation 'for cyclists and travellers. Apply Miss Myerscough'.

Photograph: London Borough of Hillingdon

## THE LOWLY HERD COMES . . .

Ickenham's Long Lane in about 1909, today a very busy main road
lined with detached Metro-land villas and planted with flowering
trees. This kind of rural scene could be found within a short distance
of many Metro-land stations fifty or sixty years ago.

Photograph: Authors' Collection

## NEW HOMES FOR SALE

Pay £15 down and then 8*s* 6*d* a week . . . and you could be the proud owner of a home in Metro-land at Ruislip Manor or Ickenham. This picture vividly depicts the transition from country to suburb. Soon the shaddy oak tree will be felled for a second row of houses, then the grass cleared for another road behind. Yet although mass-production methods were being used for 1930s domestic building, horse-drawn transport was still in evidence. The cart in this picture was probably one of William Clark's, the Ruislip haulier. He owned a large 'fleet' of horses and carts and carried most of the bricks for the Manor Homes Estates from the Metropolitan yard at Ruislip station.

Photograph: London Borough of Hillingdon

## UXBRIDGE TRANSFORMING

In the Victorian era Uxbridge had been a country town; thought it had its own industries, its development had been hampered by lack of direct rail communication with London. All this changed in 1904/5. The London United Trams arrived in the High Street and the Metropolitan at Belmont Road.

Construction of the Harrow and Uxbridge Railway began in 1901 and the station and goods yard at Uxbridge are shown here under construction by Bott and Stennell. The steam 'Navvy' on the right of the picture was one of three used along the line. Supplies of gravel were obtained from a lake at Hundred Acres Farm, Denham. The station building at Uxbridge was lit by electricity from the start, but Ruislip (then the only intermediate station) was oil-lit until the start of electric traction in 1905.

Photograph: Authors' Collection

## UXBRIDGE GOODS YARD

One of the locomotives in this picture from 1904 is an 'E' class engine. The road of houses in the distance is Belmont Road. The new Uxbridge station was opened on a re-alignment in 1938, conveniently sited in the middle of the High Street.

Photograph: Authors' Collection

## WAITING FOR THE TRAIN

These local dignitaries waiting for the official opening train on 30 June 1904 include Charles Woodbridge and Alfred Button, both local businessmen, and A. Bailey, the MP for Uxbridge. Also present were Sir Frances Dixon-Hart and Colonel F. Cox, the owner of Harefield Place. When the train arrived, the parties gathered for speeches and then moved to a large marquee near the station yard for a commemorative repast provided by Mrs Flood of 'The Chequers', sitting down to salmon, ham, veal, tongue, pigeon pie, beef and lamb, pine creams, fruit and cheese, washed down with many glasses of best hock, claret and celebration champagne. The toast was given by Colonel J.J. Mellow, who remarked that Uxbridge had stood still for half a century until that day.

Photograph: Authors' Collection

## THE TUBE COMES TO UXBRIDGE

Soon after the Metropolitan Railway became part of London Transport in 1933, the Piccadilly line from Hammersmith to South Harrow was extended to Uxbridge. This picture shows the terminus on the morning of 23 October 1933. One of the first tube trains is standing beside a set of Metropolitan 'Bogie' electric stock. The destination on the Piccadilly Line train is interesting. 'East Barnet' was the proposed name for what is now Oakwood. The name 'East Barnet' was never used, the station opening on 13th March 1933 as Enfield West. Notice, too, that the positive electric rail is sited close to the station platform — a feature dating from the early days of electrification.

Photograph: London Borough of Hillingdon

# BORDER COUNTRY

## NORTH HARROW TO WATFORD AND RICKMANSWORTH

## SUBURBIA COMES TO HARROW

Just look at the prices of the houses advertised on the bridge! But, after all, it is 1933, and more and more people were coming to settle in North Harrow. Estate developers offered special terms for 'Civil servants and bank officers'.

The original Metropolitan halt was opened in 1915 near the hamlet of Hooking Green. The railway bridge, which originally ran over a cart track (transformed in the picture into a suburban main road) was rebuilt and the steel carrying the tracks rolled into position on 17 November 1929; the new station buildings came into service in 1931. The buses are working routes 230 (Northwick Park to North Harrow via Wealdstone) and 353 (North Harrow to Pinner via Hatch End), on which the maximum fare was 4*d*. The vehicles are Dennis Darts and Guy Victory types. North Harrow shops at this time included S.H. Williams — 'electrical and wireless engineer -- accumulators charged' — and S.S. Learmouth — 'home-made toffee 4oz for 4*d*. We have the finest soda fountain in the district -- opposite North Harrow station by Headstone Hotel.'

Photograph: Authors' Collection

**THE RAILWAY REACHES PINNER**
Whit Monday 25 May 1885 and the first train arrives, pulled by a 'B' type Beyer Peacock locomotive (probably Number 65 or 66).

Photograph: London Borough of Harrow

# Cecil Park Estate,
## PINNER.

*(The property of the Metropolitan Railway Surplus Lands Committee.)*

Rent, £50 or £55.

GOOD CLASS SEMI-DETACHED HOUSES to be LET. Rents from £50 to £75.

PLOTS OF LAND
 for the erection of Houses of good class are also to be let on Building Lease at moderate ground rents.

THIS ESTATE
 is beautifully timbered, charmingly situated, and is within a few minutes walk of Pinner Village and of the Metropolitan Railway Station.

**THE CECIL PARK ESTATE**
Not long after the line was opened the Metropolitan Surplus Lands Committee began work on the Cecil Park housing estate, and a number of these stately houses were built.

Photograph: Authors' Collection

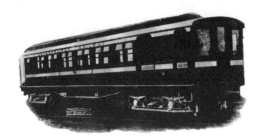

## PINNER SIGNAL BOX
A typical Metropolitan signal box on the extension line at the end of the nineteenth century. In the background work is progressing on the Cecil Park housing estate.

Photograph: Authors' Collection

### PINNER FAIR

One of the traditions of 'inner' Metro-land was Pinner's famous street fair, held each year on the Wednesday after Whitsun since the days of King John in the ancient High Street (little altered today). At the top, beside the church, stood The Cocoa Tree Tavern, opened in 1878 in a building designed by the distinguished nineteenth-century architects Ernest George and Peto. This was no usual tavern; its owner, Judge Barber, was a teetotaller and the beverages served were coffee, tea and cocoa. The tavern sign depicted a tree from which hung cups of cocoa. 'The Cocoa Tree — the ideal pleasure resort for home-made cakes and strawberry teas,' ran the advertisement in the *Metro-land* guide. The tavern closed in 1931.

Photograph: Authors' Collection

# CUCKOO HILL ESTATE, PINNER

8 minutes' walk from Pinner Station (Metro.)

## THE CITY MAN'S IDEAL RESIDENTIAL SUBURB

AN IDEAL TYPE ON THE ESTATE.

## SUPERIOR FREEHOLD VILLAS AND SPACIOUS BUILDING PLOTS FOR SALE

Room for Garage. Houses built to your own ideas and designs. Government Guaranteed Title. Good Road. Main Drainage. Gas, Water, Electricity. Mortgages arranged. Expert advice on all matters. Good Schools. Tennis Courts are on the Estate. Inspection cordially invited.

Write for Brochure to **W. A. TELLING, LTD.**

**CUCKOO HILL ESTATE OFFICE, STATION APPROACH, PINNER**

TEL.: PINNER 598

## EASTCOTE END PARK ESTATE :: EASTCOTE
(Close to Eastcote Station)

Attractive 3-Bedroom Houses and Bungalows. Write for full Particulars to :

**W. A. TELLING, Ltd., Estate Office, Eastcote Stn.** TEL.: PINNER 210

SAY YOU SAW IT IN "METRO-LAND."

Page 122

**CUCKOO HILL**

Detached houses set in leafy lanes were the style of housing developments in the Pinner area. Big gardens, bowling greens, tennis courts and rock gardens were the vogue. Cuckoo Hill was a 1930s development very popular with City businessmen.

Photograph: Authors' Collection

## NORTHWOOD HILLS

The economic troubles of the 1930s brought many northern builders down to London to try their luck in the rapidly-expanding suburbs. Northwood Hills was largely the product of one such businessman. He purchased acres of local land in 1931, and a board appeared in rural Joel Street proclaiming 'Site for new station. Frequent trains to London, City and West End'.

At Northwood Hills C.W. Clark designed another of his 'suburban villa' stations, which was opened in 1933, and soon the houses began to rise along Joel Street and the Pinner Road. Note the typically muddy early suburban roadway.

Photograph: London Borough of Hillingdon

## GOLF AND A DISTINCTIVE RESIDENCE

The great mansion of Moor Park and its extensive grounds were sold after the First World War and purchased by Lord Leverhulme for housing development and an extensive golf course. The new housing was advertised as 'The Gateway to the Chilterns', although Rickmansworth was really the geographical gateway.

Photograph: Authors' Collection

TYPICAL VIEW ON THE MOOR PARK ESTATE.

IN Metro-land—London's nearest countryside—you will find all that you can reasonably ask. It has character and charm; variety and interest. It is the most accessible and least spoiled residential district around London and its train service is the envy of all. There are Through trains to and from the City both morning and evening; there are " non-stop " trains, " cheap " trains, " theatre " trains—everything in fact that you can possibly desire.

But this is not all. Metro-land lays definite claim to be the most healthy district around London. The climate is mild and equable: the air is clean and invigorating and the subsoil, for the most part, is gravel. There are unlimited facilities for outdoor recreation; there are sixteen golf courses from which to choose; educational and shopping facilities are exceptionally liberal, whilst the Season Ticket rates will be found within the reach of all.

The residential districts nearest at hand are Wembley Park, Northwick Park and Harrow. Then comes Rayners Lane, immediately serving the delightful Harrow Garden Village, followed by Eastcote, Ruislip and Uxbridge. Further afield, yet still within easy reach, are Pinner, Northwood, Moor Park, Rickmansworth and Chorley Wood. Beyond these are Chesham, Amersham and Great Missenden, and then, as a fitting climax, comes Wendover—a gem of rural scenery.

The Publicity Manager, London Passenger Transport Board, 55, Broadway, Westminster, S.W.1, will gladly afford every assistance to those in search of a house and cordially invites particulars of their requirements when he will be happy to furnish information of appropriate property.

# MOOR PARK ESTATE

## *TWENTY-FIVE MINUTES FROM TOWN*

**Frequent through expresses to and from the City.**

The Estate is an unspoiled historic old English park, being developed in a manner to preserve and protect its delightful scenery, and thus combine the facilities of London with the rural amenities of the County of Hertford.

| MAIN DRAINAGE | SAND and GRAVEL SUBSOIL |

**Price FREEHOLD £2,225**

**Price FREEHOLD £2,275**

| ELECTRIC LIGHT | GAS CONNECTED |

*The above are typical examples of the houses erected and in course of erection at Moor Park, designed in the inexpensive efficient style of modern architecture, blending utility of accommodation with attractiveness of elevation.*

### ILLUSTRATIONS AND PLANS OF THESE AND OTHER HOUSES AT MOOR PARK

*contained in a booklet which also describes the three eighteen hole golf courses, magnificent Club House, tennis courts, etc.*

### MAY BE HAD ON APPLICATION

*by letter, phone or a personal visit to the Estate, from the*

## Estate Manager, Moor Park, HERTS
*Phone : Rickmansworth 217.*

## MOOR PARK ADVERTISING

'Here one may enjoy quietude and seclusion (without isolation) with all the amenities of residence in an old English park, yet without the responsibility of its ownership. Houses cost from £1,000. Plots from £4 10s a foot.' There were 'frequent electric expresses to the City; 25 minutes from Baker Street'. First-Class season tickets to the City (who would have travelled any other class from Moor Park?!) cost £7 17s 6d a quarter. In the elegant classical hall of the great house at any time on a weekend afternoon, golfing residents would be taking tea and discussing the latest game. This was Metro-land life at its best. Tennis courts, leafy avenues, bridge parties, velvet lawns. Even the roads were private.

Photograph: Authors' Collection

## THE WATFORD BRANCH

One of the original plans for the Watford branch had included an embankment across Cassiobury Park and a terminus in the middle of the town. After the First World War the plans were modified and a shorter route was constructed, with the station near the park. Though the line was a joint venture with the L.N.E.R., the L.N.E.R. was reluctant to put money into it.

This picture shows the line being built south of Croxley Green, with workmen hard at work on the deep cutting. The bridge carries Harvey Road over the line. The contractors were Logan and Hemmingway, and they had a very difficult task cutting through the chalk. The total cost of the line was £387,000.

Photograph: Authors' Collection

## OPENING DAY AT CROXLEY

The date is 31 October 1925; the time is 12.18, and this is the official opening train with Metropolitan-Vickers electric locomotive 'Sarah Siddons'. The special train had left Baker Street at 11.50, carrying Lord Faringdon (Deputy Chairman L.N.E.R.) and Lord Aberconway (Chairman of the Metropolitan). The second vehicle is the celebrated Rothschild Saloon. There appears to be some trouble with a leaking steam pipe towards the rear of the train.

Public services began on 2 November 1925, and the *Watford Observer* said: 'The Metropolitan Railway extension to Watford, opened on Saturday, is likely to have a much greater effect on the development of the town that is at present realized. Just as trade follows the flag, so population follows the railway.' Though the L.N.E.R. passenger services to Marylebone were never resumed after the General Strike in 1926, the houses soon came. The *Metro-land* guide for 1931 said: 'Cassiobury Park, which for long automatically checked expansion of Watford on the north-west side, is now its chief encouragement to residential expansion, for the historic mansion, and the park of the Earls of Essex have succumbed to the irrestistible pressure of the times, and deep fringes of the park on this side have already been converted to building sites.'

Photograph: Authors' Collection

## BY BUS TO TOWN

The Metropolitan had four of these 28-seater Albion buses which took passengers into the centre of the town via Vicarage Road and Watford High Street. There was a flat fare of 1*d*, and the circular route began operation on 2 November 1927. Later the buses were run by the North West Land and Transport company, a Metropolitan subsidiary. After 1929 the route was operated by the Lewis Omnibus Company, although the fleet name 'Metropolitan' was retained.

Photograph: Borough of Watford

**WATFORD HIGH STREET, 1926**
The building where the word 'Restaurant' is just visible was intended
to be the Metropolitan's Watford terminus. There was even a short
strip of land behind wide enough for the railway tracks. But the
scheme never materialized; the building was opened as the Empress
Restaurant and Winter Gardens and today it is the Grange
Furnishing Company.

Photograph: Authors' Collection

## NEW TRAINS FOR WATFORD

An 'MV' compartment stock train (later 'T' stock) in rural Metro-land days. The 'MV' cars were built for the Watford service and were delivered in 1927. With later types of compartment stock, these trains continued to serve Watford until 5 October 1962.

Photograph: London Transport

## THE GATEWAY TO THE CHILTERNS

Despite the advertisers' claim that Moor Park was the gateway, it was really Rickmansworth. Here the electric lines ended, and the Metropolitan-Vickers electric locomotives were changed for steam ready for the long, slow climb up through the beech woods to Chorley Wood and the Chiltern Hills. The locomotive change was said to be the fastest on any railway in the world. This picture shows 'John Hampden' entering the station in about 1950. Note the variety of signals, the wooden signal cabin and also the modern colour lights which were about to replace the old equipment. On the left is the end of the bay line, from which the shuttle train used to run round to Croxley and Watford.

Photograph: C.R.L. Coles

## STEAM DAYS AT RICKMANSWORTH

Metropolitan 'H' class locomotive with train of 'Dreadnought' carriages entering the station in 1932. Rickmansworth was a popular place for excursions; there were the beautiful grounds of Chesswater Estate 'opened by Mr Wilson Young on Wednesdays and Thursdays', walks along the canal towpath to see the narrow boats being worked through the locks, a ramble down the Colne valley to Harefield Lock, or the delights of the River Chess. Teas with Zeeta and Kunzle cakes were offered by local shops such as Beasleys and at 'Ye Old Red Spider' for 1s6d.

Photograph: London Transport

## WAITING FOR DUTY

Beside the old goods shed at Rickmansworth in the early 1950s, Metropolitan-Vickers locomotives 'Michael Faraday' and 'Edmund Burke' await their turn to take a train south to Baker Street.

Photograph: C.R.L. Coles

VIEW ON THE CEDARS ESTATE

## HOW TO PURCHASE OUT OF INCOME

A PROPERTY, or Site alone, can be acquired on easy terms of payment, and the following is an example :—

| | | |
|---|---|---|
| Purchase Price | - - - - | £725 |
| Cash deposit | - - - - | £25 |
| Balance | - - - - | £700 |

to be paid over a period of 20 years in quarterly sums, with interest at £6 per cent. per annum.

£700 over 20 years = £35 0 0 per annum or £8 15 0 per quarter.

| **1st Payment.** | | **3rd Payment.** | |
|---|---|---|---|
| Principal—1 Quarter - | £8 15 0 | Principal—1 Quarter - | £8 15 0 |
| £6% p.a. Interest on £700 for 3 months - - | £10 10 0 | £6% p.a. Interest on £682 10 0 for 3 months | £10 4 9 |
| | £19 5 0 | | £18 19 9 |
| **2nd Payment.** | | **4th Payment.** | |
| Principal—1 Quarter - | £8 15 0 | Principal—1 Quarter - | £8 15 0 |
| £6% p.a. Interest on £691 5 0 for 3 months | £10 7 5 | £6% p.a. Interest on £673 15 0 for 3 months | £10 2 2 |
| | £19 2 5 | | £18 17 2 |

And so on from quarter, the quarterly amount of principal remaining the same, but the interest diminishing as the principal is paid off.

**Alternatively,** the balance of £700 can be paid on a "flat" rate of £15 4 6 per quarter throughout the 20 years.

In either case the period of years can be reduced and the deposit increased, according to the requirements of a purchaser, in which case the rate of interest is suitably lowered.

NOTE.—The prices quoted include architect's fees, fencing, the cost of the area of the land stated, and the property decorated for occupation.

Page Two

# CEDARS ESTATE
## RICKMANSWORTH
### HERTFORDSHIRE

## IDYLLIC COUNTRY LIFE

Advertisement for the Cedars Estate, 'an exceptionally attractive residential country estate, comprising over 600 acres of beautiful undulating country, rising to an altitude of over 300 feet, with a subsoil of gravel and chalk, and adjoining the old-world country town of Rickmansworth and extending westwards to Chorley Wood.'

Photograph: Authors' Collection

## BUT CAN WE AFFORD IT?

You could buy a 'specially designed detached residence which embraces all modern and labour-saving conveniences' for £975, while a luxury detached house was available at £2,150. If you had the money all you had to do was ring H. Gibson at The Metropolitan Railway Country Estates head office or their local office at Meadow Way.

Photograph: Authors' Collection

# THE CHESS VALLEY

## CHORLEY WOOD TO CHESHAM

## EARLY DAYS ON THE EXTENSION LINE

Chesham-bound train between Rickmansworth and Chorley Wood. The locomotive is one of the fairly short-lived 'C' class built by Nelson and Co. in 1891. These engines were similar to the 'Q' class then being built by the same company for the South Eastern Railway of which Sir Edward Watkin was Chairman. The 'C' class were designed with condensing apparatus for working the tunnels in London.

Photograph: H.C. Casserley Collection

## SOUTHBOUND FREIGHT

Freight trains such as this were a familiar sight to Metropolitan travellers. Much of the traffic on this train was probably intended for transhipment to the Midland line at Finchley Road. The locomotive is one of the 'K' class built by Armstrong Whitworth and Co. in 1924. The oil-lit platforms carry the sign 'Chorley Wood and Chenies'; the name Chenies was added in November 1915.

Chorley Wood was a favourite spot for outings. The building on the right of the picture is the Chorley Wood Hotel, where Mr Grimmer dispensed luncheon for 2s 6d and offered 'ample accommodation for motor cars'. Children could enjoy themselves on the breezy common or sample Younger's Retreat, where there were swings, toys and donkeys, to say nothing of watercress teas. And in the 1930s the more go-ahead families could stay at Stagg Farm Holiday Camp, where tents or huts were available (with all meals) from Saturday lunchtime to Sunday evening for 7s 6d.

Photograph: H.C. Casserley Collection

## THE OLD BERKELEY (WEST) HOUNDS

This was a scene often met by early visitors to Metro-land. The meet here, one day in April 1930, prepares to leave Chalfont St. Giles village, having gathered before the 'Merlin's Cave' at the green. The large group of villagers, including the inevitable small boys, stand at a respectful distance while some of the huntsmen, including one watering his horse at the pond, have yet to join. During the 1930s, the waters of the river Misbourne (in the background) failed and tended to give weight to the old Chilterns' folklore that the river disappeared under the chalk when some national crisis was approaching.

Photograph: County Museum Aylesbury

## LONGBOTTOM LANE, CHALFONT

Even as late as 1935, when this picture was taken, rural transport has changed little and walkers were seldom bothered by traffic on the small country roads. The year's harvest is being gathered in; the cornfield has been cut by a reaper-binder machine and the stocks of wheat collected to await transport by horse and cart to the farm. Some time later, a visiting threshing machine will complete the full operation today performed by the combine-harvester as the cereal is cut. Although farming had come a long way by the 1930s from the labour-intensive days of hand-reaping, farm labourers worked long hours, loading well into the night. The horse in this scene appears to have been taken around its harness so that it can stand away from the afternoon sun.

Photograph: County Museum Aylesbury

## CHANGE HERE FOR CHESHAM

The London platform at Chalfont & Latimer, with the Chesham train waiting for the arrival of the next 'up' train on the main line. It is an afternoon in about 1930, and the young man in the picture is dressed in his Saturday morning City office attire. Now he waits, no doubt contemplating the prospect of an enjoyable Chiltern weekend. The locomotive is Number 81 'E' class, built by Hawthorn Leslie in 1900/1. the train is composed of 1910 'Dreadnought' carriages.

Photograph: H.C. Casserley Collection

## BUILDING THE LINE

Contractor's locomotive 'Groombridge' and navvy gang mid-way between Chesham and Chalfont Road (the original name for Chalfont & Latimer) in about 1887. The branch had a number of tight curves as it descended to the Chess valley. Originally the Met had planned a terminus some way out of the town, but the local people raised the money to buy land so that the station could be near the town centre.

Photograph: Authors' Collection

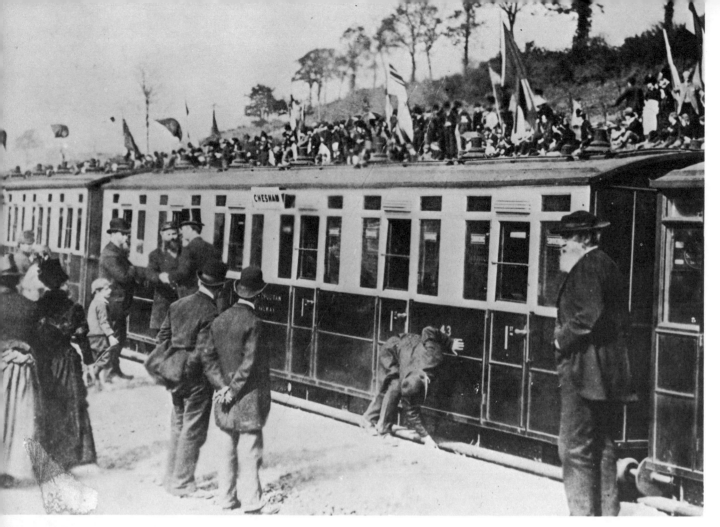

## BIG DAY AT CHESHAM

'Long live the Queen and Teddy Watkin' shouted the crowds at Chesham on 8 July 1889, when the official opening train drew to a halt. While officials directed their attention to welcoming the directors of the Metropolitan Railway, an orderly stoops down, squeezing his hand dangerously between the running-board and the platform edge. Has his official invitation card been lost, or has part of the running board worked loose? We shall never know. The coaches are some of the original Metropolitan 'straight' top door stock of the 1860s.

Photograph: London Transport

## CHESHAM STATION, 1933

Locomotive Number 1 'E' class of 1898 has just drawn into the single platform with a 'Dreadnought' stock train. The engine was used for the official opening train on the Harrow & Uxbridge line in 1904 and is now preserved at the Quainton Road Railway Centre. The signal box is still there — but without the advertisements — and the station has changed little, though the once extensive goods yards have now become car parks.

Photograph: H.C. Casserley Collection

**LORD'S MILL, CHESHAM, 1932**

One of the last mill buildings in Metro-land, astride the Chess. A coal merchant and his horse-drawn cart make their leisurely way around the town, the driver singing out his current prices for a hundredweight sack of coal to catch the impulse-buying housewife. The coal would have been loaded at the Metropolitan's Chesham Yard. Lord's Mill had a huge undershot wheel which disappeared in 1900 when mechanical power was introduced.

Photograph: County Museum Aylesbury

## THE SATURDAY LUNCHTIME PULLMAN

The London shops have closed, the banks have locked their massive doors and the warm spring sunshine means the Chilterns. Here the Chesham Saturday lunchtime Pullman leaves the main line to take the branch just beyond Chalfont in the early 1930s. The First World War has sprinkled the Chilterns with memorials and it is still a little uncertain what is happening in Germany. But it's Saturday and time to forget economic troubles at home. Pack the picnic bag with the Thermos, the bloater paste sandwiches and the coconut macaroons, the Bakelite cups and those funny little knives with artificial bone handles. And don't forget the portable gramophone so that we can listen to Paul Whiteman and that new man Crosby.

Photograph: H.C. Casserley Collection

# WALKERS' METRO~LAND

## AMERSHAM TO AYLESBURY

## A WEEKEND IN METRO-LAND

Pulling hard up the gradient, filled with homeward-bound City clerks (and managers) all looking forward to a weekend of golf or time with the 'kiddies' in the newly-built houses amid the beech woods, comes the Aylesbury train. The locomotive is one of Charles Jones's fine 'H' class engines of 1920. Its sides were resplendent in crimson lake livery, with the gold of the Metropolitan Railway coat-of-arms. Behind the engine are the teak finished 'Dreadnought' carriages, with their roomy First-Class compartments, among the most comfortable on any suburban line out of London. This picture is the very quintessence of Metro-land.

Photograph: London Transport

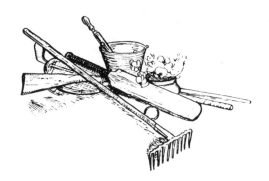

## FAST TRAIN TO BAKER STREET

Amersham station in April 1935. The footbridge is a typical Met lattice type but more unusually has a covered top and glass screen. The locomotive is 'H' class Number 107.

It was not until the 1900s that the first ambitious housing developments took place around Amersham station. The new community incorporated Chesham Bois — hence the station nameplate. Old Amersham down in the Misbourne valley offered plenty of interest for the visitor. One of the popular Metro-land views was from the wood that lies between Amersham-on-the-Hill and the old town. There were many ancient inns and also more go-ahead places such as The Crown, where you could dance the fox-trot to an 'electric radio-gramophone'.

Photograph: H.C. Casserley Collection

**LATIMER** The village was a familiar sight to walkers in the 1930s. The oblong cairn, above the War Memorial and the pump, marks the spot where the horse of Boer War General de Villebois Marcevill was buried. It was said that the General saved the life of his enemy, Lord Chesham, during the South African War. So this is a curious tribute to a brave adversary.

**GREAT MISSENDEN HIGH STREET, 1903**
The long village street built in early Victorian times changed only gradually. The pavements are cobbled, and the carriageway is fouled with horse droppings where the delivery carts stand near the kerb. An old countryman makes his horse ready as his daughters sit in the family dog-cart — the equivalent of today's 'mini' — while another villager, perhaps on his way to an allotment, trundles his wheelbarrow (complete with spade) in the centre of the road with complete abandon.

Photograph: Authors' Collection

### GREAT HAMPDEN PARK LODGES
These pretty little one-storey brick lodge houses, well known to walkers in Metro-land west of Great Missenden, stand at the foot of the long avenue leading to Hampden House. It is said that the drive was cut to allow Queen Elizabeth I and her retinue to reach the original house by a direct way. This photograph was probably taken in the spring one year in the 1920s. The lodges were always known locally as the 'pepperpots', because of their squat circular shape.

Photograph: Authors' Collection

**CLIMBING DUTCHLANDS SUMMIT**

A typical Metroplitan main line scene in the 1930s. The locomotive is Number 116 of the 'K' class. The wagons contained bricks and timber for the new housing estates of 'inner' Metro-land. In the distance can be seen the woods on Halton Hill which were then growing up following replanting after the First World War; German prisoners of war had felled the original timbers.

Photograph: C.R.L. Coles

## WENDOVER HIGH STREET

Early afternoon about 1911 in that peaceful Metro-land before the Great War. The old shepherd has been made to pose in rustic fashion, standing stiffly self-conscious right in the middle of the street. But after all it is unlikely that the local car will suddenly rattle round the bend, and all the cyclists are in London at their office desks. Nobody else is around, except for the two small boys, who seem to be regarding the old man as a sort of performing animal! Two little girls in white smocks stare from the distance. In the background, behind the clock tower, are the dark woods of Halton. In a few years time the trees will all be felled.

The poet Rupert Brooke came to Wendover in these years and climbed Coombe Hill:

> The Roman road to Wendover,
> By Tring and Lilley Hoo.

From the high ridges he looked out over the Vale to Aylesbury — the open fields of undeveloped Metro-land:

> White mist about the black hedgerows,
> The slumbering Midland plain,
> The silence where the clover grows,
> And the dead leaves in the lane.

Photograph: County Museum Aylesbury

## THE HORSE-BOX

The Metropolitan catered for the horseman as well as the commuter, and a number of horse-boxes were stationed at various points. The Wendover box van was built by G.R. Turner and Co. in 1904 and survived until 1938.

Photograph: H.C. Casserley Collection

## ON MAIN-LINE SERVICE

The Brill branch was worked by veteran Beyer Peacock locomotives 23 and 41. Here the photographer has caught Number 23 hurrying through the Chilterns near Wendover with a goods train many miles from its usual haunts. It was a common practice to attach wagons to the engines when they were making their regular trips down to Neasden and back for routine maintenance.

Photograph: H.C. Casserley Collection

## METRO-LAND ROMANTICIZED

A cottage at Stoke Mandeville in about 1908. This is the romantic image of the Chilterns that the literature of the Metropolitan Railway sought to pass on to an urban public used to slums and overcrowding. Life was as hard for the countryman as for his brother who had left to seek work in the town, but it was scenes such as this of old cottages, wobbly stiles, fieldpaths and streams that made Metro-land so attractive in the 1920s and 1930s for a day in the country and encouraged the ideal of a weekend rural life.

Photograph: Authors' Collection

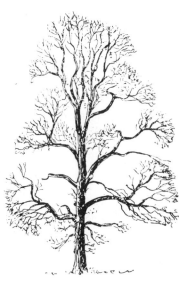

## FINAL DAYS OF THE PASSENGER TANKS

The locomotive in charge of this train coming into Stoke Mandeville is an 'H' class of 1920 but running with L.N.E.R. on the sides and with a new number, 6421. The larger Metropolitan engines were sold to the L.N.E.R. in 1937 and for the most part ended their lives in such distant places as Colwick and Annesley in Nottinghamshire.

The station gardens at Stoke Mandeville were among the most attractive on the Metropolitan extension line in the 1930s.

Photograph: H.C. Casserley Collection

## CUTTING THE FIRST SOD

It was a bleak and windy day when the crowds gathered to watch the first sod for the Metropolitan Railway extension into Aylesbury being dug out in about 1890. The contractor's foreman waits to take the barrow with its sample of important earth. Everyone, except the inquisitive woman from the far cottage (who has dashed out to be recorded for posterity), wears a hat, cap or bonnet.

Photograph: County Museum Aylesbury

## THE FIRST TRAIN

On 1 September 1892, at 10.45am, the first through train to Aylesbury left Baker Street and, after years of negotiations and proposals, the county town at last had a direct railway service to London. At the inaugural luncheon an important guest was ninety-three-year-old Sir Harry Verney, who had tried so hard to get this important connection to London built.

Photograph: County Museum Aylesbury

## RIVAL ROUTES TO LONDON

Aylesbury station on 2 May 1936: a L.N.E.R. express for Marylebone is about to leave, while an 'H' class Metropolitan locomotive waits with a Baker Street train on the right. The Great Central expresses soon found that the steeply-graded and busy Metropolitan route through the Chilterns and down to Harrow (with only twin tracks) was difficult to work. The opening of the Great Central line via Ashendon, then joint with the G.W.R. via Princes Risborough to Northolt Junction, and from there round to Neasden via Sudbury, was a longer but much more convenient route. The Great Central only ran express services at first; its suburban service on the Metropolitan route began in March 1906, and posters announced 'The Great Central Railway is the Line of Health.'

Photograph: H.C. Casserley Collection

# INSPECTION
### OF
# AYLESBURY EXTENSION,
### SEPTEMBER 1st 1892.

## Special Train Arrangements.

| DOWN. | A.M. | UP. | P.M. |
|---|---|---|---|
| BAKER ST. EAST | 10 45 | AYLESBURY | 4 20 |
| HARROW | 11 8 | STOKE MANDEVILLE | 4 26 |
| CHALFONT ROAD | 11 31 | WENDOVER | 4 32 |
| AMERSHAM | 11 36 | GREAT MISSENDEN | 4 41 |
| GREAT MISSENDEN | 11 46 | AMERSHAM | 4 51 |
| WENDOVER | 11 55 | CHALFONT ROAD | 4 58 |
| STOKE MANDEVILLE | 11 59 | HARROW | 5 20 |
| AYLESBURY | 12 5 | BAKER ST. EAST | 5 38 |

## DISASTER AT CHRISTMAS

Daylight on 23 December 1904 at Aylesbury showed smashed carriages and buildings and the locomotive of the 2.45am parcels train from Marylebone on its side at the Joint station. In dense fog, the Marylebone train, heading north, had jumped the line at a bend and run on to plough up the platform. Carriages were telescoped, and the driver, who was thrown from his engine, died later. A signalman at the subsequent enquiry stated that the train was travelling at 50 mph on the curve, where speed was limited to 15 mph. He said to his mate in the signal box, 'It's a licker to me if she gets round the corner all right.'

Three companies (G.C.R., G.W.R. and Metropolitan) ran their trains into Aylesbury Joint station, which was alleged to have been 'none too convenient at the best of times'. The crash would have been worse but for the swift action of the signalman and a fogman, who ran forward to place a detonator on the line in the path of an express from the north. The signalman moved his levers as the train roared by. 'I felt death was upon me, Sir,' he confessed at the enquiry.

One of the vans of the Marylebone train disgorged its cargo of Christmas puddings across the lines, and it wasn't long before the local people were 'helping to clear the track'.

Photograph: County Museum Aylesbury

# ACROSS THE VALLEY

## AYLESBURY TO QUAINTON ROAD

## WADDESDON MANOR STATION

This scene, taken from the foot of the steps on the 'down' platform at Waddesdon Manor, is thought by Mr John Reed of Aylesbury to have been taken in 1906, 1907 or 1908. There are few photographic reminders of this station, just under five miles from Aylesbury, which was built by the Metropolitan Railway at the time when the Met had removed the level-crossings between Aylesbury and the terminus at Verney Juntion and replaced them with bridges.

The London-bound express in the photograph is hauled by Number 260, built in early 1906. The coaches are in a two-tone colour, abandoned by the Great Central in favour of a teak finish in 1908. The signals are Metropolitan type, with balancing weights beyond the spectacle glass. The milk churns are likely to be empties; milk traffic was to build up on the Met as the suburbs expanded and the unpleasant habit of keeping a cow or two for milking in a London yard was abandoned. Waddesdon Station was unusual for Metropolitan Railway design in that the main buildings were on the 'down' side, and its standard-type waiting-hut on the 'up'.

Photograph: Authors' Collection

102

## LAST DAYS AT WADDESDON
Time and the camera have moved on and it is now 1936. The L.N.E.R. rail motor, with locomotive at the rear, is on its way to Verney Junction. Soon the station will be closed and the buildings boarded up. Grass will cover the platforms and by the 1970s only the platforms will be left.

Photograph: Authors' Collection

## WHADDON HOUNDS

This picture, taken in 1933, is full of the feeling of a winter's day, as a fitful splash of early-morning sunshine patches its way through rolling country mists and the frost bewitches every long blade of roadside grass into a white curve of candy-floss. Even the dogs look mildly worried, and the third man plods carefully beside his horse.

The Hunt still survives today and from time to time finds that its interests conflict with those of householders, as urban development spreads out from Aylesbury.

Photograph: County Museum Aylesbury

## THE 'CLAPHAM JUNCTION' OF METRO-LAND

Plans for a great 'Clapham Junction' (as Sir John Betjeman has described it) at Quainton Road never materialized. Metropolitan trains never reached Northampton or Oxford, although the goods yard did flourish with interchange traffic between the Metropolitan and the Great Central.

In this picture the mixed train for Brill simmers on the right with the Beyer-Peacock veteran Number 41 locomotive. The L.N.E.R. rail-motor is 'parked' on a siding, and long lines of wagons stand in the left background.

Today Quainton Road is the headquarters of the Quainton Railway Society.

Photograph: London Transport

## WHEELWRIGHT'S AT QUAINTON

Quainton village lies some half mile away from the station. Nothing disturbs the pace of country life in these mid-Buckinghamshire villages, and this scene of the wheelwright's cottage is, to all purposes, the same as can be found today. Neat thatch marks the inbred tidiness of a true countryman, and old women gossip over the roses as the wheelwright's latest repairs lie outside in the sun to await their owner's return with his pony.

The villagers might have gone as far as Aylesbury on a Metropolitan train, but few would have ventured to London. Even summer hikers were greeted with amused stares, one pedestrian recalls, and cycling clubs were jeered.

Photograph: County Museum Aylesbury

QUAINTON, BUCKS. THE WHEELWRIGHTS.

## LAST DAY FOR VERNEY JUNCTION

These two studies were photographed at Quainton Road on 4 July 1936, the official closing day of the Verney passenger service. Note that the train also includes a cattle wagon. Who are the people? The bowler-hatted gent could have been a commercial traveller. But more likely he has come home from his office in Aylesbury. The schoolgirls on the opposite platform may have come home earlier from one of the big schools in Aylesbury and been told to come back to the station to watch the last trains.

Photograph: Authors' Collection

# THE BRILL 'TRAM'

## QUAINTON ROAD TO BRILL

## OFF TO BRILL

It is summer 1935 and there's not much time left if you want to ride on the little Brill train. Here the ancient engine and coach puff away from Quainton Road and round the curve to continue down the flat, straight section to Waddesdon Road.

Once it had left the main line, the Brill train pursued its leisurely way, the occasional passenger dropping off or climbing on the train as it stopped at the level-crossings. The guard and the fireman got down to work the gates. Sometimes, in early days, an informal stop would be made along the line, and the crew would set out across the fields for a while, making, no doubt, for a secret rendezvous with a mug of ale.

Photograph: Authors' Collection

## WADDESDON ROAD

Waddesdon Road in about 1934, simply a halt beside the main Aylesbury to Bicester Road. Metropolitan locomotive Number 23 approaches, one of the two engines used on the branch. One engine was kept in steam at a time. A rota was kept so that one engine left for Neasden for maintenance on Friday and returned to Quainton Road on the following Monday. The coal used was either hard Welsh steam coal (Tredegar Co.) or general purpose Bolsover Nuts, supplied by Stephenson Clarke. Drivers earned a coal consumption bonus based on mileage to coal consumed. Even here there is a short siding for coal and for local farmers to load their produce — the original purpose of the country lines.

Photograph: H.C. Casserley Collection

## WESTCOTT, 1974

One of the few tangible remains of the Brill branch are the station house and booking-hut at Westcott. This recent picture shows the site of the line looking towards Quainton; the track passed between the house and the shed. Near the station was a siding that served a small gas works. Before these were built, it had extended up to Waddesdon Hill and had been used to take the building materials for the erection of Waddesdon House.

## WESTCOTT, 1933

The siding in this picture was provided for a couple of wagons used by local farmers.

Photograph: Authors' Collection

## CHURCH SIDING

After passing under the Great Central Ashendon line at Wotton, where the station stood in a wood, the Brill line ran between hedges across the fields to a point by a water tower called Church Siding. This previously unpublished picture shows the end of this siding where it terminated behind the farm at Wotton Underwood. A horse was used to fly-shunt any wagon destined for the siding, which served only the village. At one time the 'branch' ran beyond the village to Kingswood siding, but as far as is known no pictures exist of this obscure part of the Brill system. It was near Church Siding that the only fatal accident on the Brill branch occurred, in March 1883. A lady's maid to the Duke of Buckingham's daughter was walking along the track with other girls after leaving the evening train from Quainton Road when the engine and carriage caught up the group. Maria Nicholls was knocked down and killed instantly. It seems difficult to see how this accident could have happened with a very slow moving train which rarely exceeded 10 mph at that spot. Perhaps it was a suicide.

Photograph: Authors' Collection

## CHURCH SIDING TODAY

Today the line up to Wotton Underwood has become a farm track.

Photograph: D.F. Edwards

## WOTTON HOUSE

This view shows the house in 1976. It stands overlooking the village and church of Wotton Underwood and was once the seat of the Duke of Buckingham & Chandos (Richard Plantagenet Campbell), who was so deeply involved in the Metropolitan Railway story. He married twice — his second marriage, contracted when he was sixty-two, lasted only four years; he died in 1889 at Chandos House, Marylebone, and was buried in Wotton Church, where long, still ranks of the Buckingham and Temple families lie in their special vault.

Photograph: R. Pigram

## SHOOTING PARTY

A major feature of the Edwardian Country House weekend was a shoot on the estate. This group of guns poses before the action. It was sport mainly for men; the ladies who were adventurous enough would have been allowed to leave the house and perhaps enjoy a picnic luncheon in the field.

Photograph: County Museum Aylesbury

Photograph: D.F. Edwards

## WOTTON CURVE, 1932 and 1974

Apart from the ridges in the grass in the later picture, who would guess that a railway line had run here? Even some of the wayside trees have gone.

Photograph: Authors' Collection

**AP 3 99**

**BRILL**

TO

WOOD SIDING.

3d. WOTTON.

4½d. WESTCOTT.

5½d. WADDESDON.

6½d QUAINTON.

**1297**

Oxford & Ay            ramroad Co.

This Ticket is is        po. the understanding
that the holder          claim for any loss,
inconvenience            ry. which may arise
from delays or a          ca: ty in the starting
or arrival of the         as. and that he will abide
by the Regulations of the Company.

This Ticket to be given up at end of journey
to the Collector. If lost the      assenger will be
liable to be        ed a  in.

**OXFORD & AYLESBURY TRAMROAD.**

NOT TRANSFERABLE
AVAILABLE ON DAY OF ISSUE ONLY

**BRILL**

BRILL      TO      BRILL

**BAKER STREET**

BAKER STREET     BAKER STREET

855     855

Fare 3/11½   **THIRD CLASS**   Fare 3/11½

**6 AU 00**

### DON'T FORGET THE TICKETS!

A selection of the tickets issued at the turn of the century for the Brill branch passenger service. A fare of 3s 11½d was certainly very cheap for a journey all the way to Baker Street.

Photograph: Authors' Collection

## WOOD SIDING, 1935

This was always a favourite spot for photographers of the Brill line. The halt was sited just where the branch passed over the G.W.R. main line to Bicester and Banbury; the bridge has only recently been dismantled. Even here there was the usual short siding — miles and miles from any settlement — where farm carts would load produce into the wagons for the journey to the London markets.

Photograph: London Transport

**BRICKWORKS SIDING**

The Brill Brickworks were served by a spur of the railway just before the terminus at Brill and were the source of much traffic over the years. Bricks from here were used in the construction of the rival Great Central spur at Wotton. The picture shows the points at the siding in about 1920. Train crews had a token with a key which unlocked the points, and the wagons were shunted by means of ropes pulled by the locomotive. The brickworks chimney can be seen in the background.

Photograph: Authors' Collection

**BRILL BRICKWORKS**
The end of the sidings in 1934. Wagons are waiting to be loaded on a
service track badly overgrown by grass.

## BRILL STATION, MARCH 1930
The end of the Metropolitan Railway's line at Brill, at one time planned to run on to Oxford. The station stood at the foot of a very long hill. At the public auction in September 1936, after the closure of the branch, the wooden water tower seen in use here fetched only £1, and the tumbledown tiled workshop behind the wagon was sold off at £1 15*s*.

Photograph: H.C. Casserley Collection

## BRILL HIGH STREET ABOUT 1910

The timetable boards exhibited beside the entrance to the 'Sun' Hotel carried the times of trains from the Brill (Met) Station and from Brill & Ludgershall Station (G.W.R.). Seaton's Private Hotel, which appears to have been prepared to cope with a flood of gentry heading for Dorton Spa, later became Newman's bakery and in 1975 the grocery shop of Messrs. Cross.

In his *Innkeeper's Diary,* John Fothergill records a customer at the 'Spread Eagle' in Thame, a nearby town, who found that he had left his hat behind after leaving the inn. In a scrambled telephone conversation all the publican could catch as a clue for restoring the hat to its owner was that the customer's cottage at Brill did not possess a bathroom. The line went dead, but the gallant publican drove over to Brill, only, alas, to be told that no house in Brill possessed a bathroom anyway. The story may now be some way from reality, but it illustrates just how remote from Baker Street and urban civilization was the Brill branch.

Photograph: County Museum Aylesbury

## DORTON SPA

About half a mile east of Brill springs of Chalybeate water were discovered and in the late 1830s an attempt was made to found a spa here. Pavilions were built to the design of a Mr Hakewell, and even in desolation, as shown in this old print from 1910, they had a charm and elegance completely out of place in this green leafy backwater of rural England. A great artificial lake was planned and there were to be regular attractions of concerts and fireworks. How different the remote Metropolitan branch to Brill would have been had royalty breathed popularity and fashion into these spectral places! In the early days the young Queen had the choice of Dorton or Leamington, and with royal favour unforthcoming the lake on which the gentry had boated and bathed sank away to return to wood; the Pump Room itself was taken down in about the early 1920s. As late as the 1840s, the proprietors, in some last attempts to save the spa, were trying *promenades musicales* and a grand *fête*. Now only the light rustle of leaves and the occasional sound of sheep in the nearby pasture disturb the solitude.

Photograph: County Museum Aylesbury

## TAKING THE WATERS

This lone adventurer samples the Dorton waters in the mid-thirties at the wooden 'beehive' in the centre of Chinkwell Wood at the invitation of the local gamekeeper. The man had scooped the crusted iron salts off the well water and plunged the mug into the pure liquid. The water tasted sharp, iron and rather unpleasant. 'It's the strongest sap in England, and only Baden is stronger in the whole of Europe,' she remembers being told. Stares and hard looks greeted the Metro-land visitor — surely one of the last to make the journey from Baker Street. The villagers were unused to visitors, and here, at Brill, she found an immense, unspoilt land, 'mile after mile of the last real country left in England'.

Photograph: Authors' Collection

## LAST TRAIN

A damp day and the end of a dream — the last daylight train at Brill, 30 November 1935. Before the closure, the Rothschild Saloon, used by the Metropolitan directors in the days of the independent company, was used to visit the line. As the train drew away from each station, documents and valuables were placed in the guard's van, and the station lights were turned out for the last time.

Photograph: Authors' Collection

# THE
# OUTERMOST FRONTIER

## QUAINTON ROAD TO VERNEY JUNCTION

## THE LINE TO VERNEY

View in the early 1930s of the junction north of Quainton Road where the Metropolitan tracks are shown here branching to the left from the Great Central main line. The train is probably being handled by one of the Metropolitan 'K' class engines built by Armstrong Whitworth and Co. in 1924.

Photograph: Authors' Collection

## . . . AND AS IT IS TODAY

Only the single-track goods line remains on the right connecting Aylesbury to the Bletchley-Bicester line via the spur at Shepherds Furze. Most of the trees in the background have survived the years.

Photograph: D.F. Edwards

## GRANBOROUGH ROAD

Granborough Road Station was set in the heart of the countryside of the Verney family. It was from country stations such as this that the Metropolitan Railway looked for income from increasing goods traffic to offset the preponderance of passenger traffic. There were no special milk trains, but a night train from Verney Junction to Baker Street had a special milk priority and picked up and delivered churns and parcels to platforms only. This train was naturally faster than the normal goods trains over this line which delivered, shunted the yard, adding and dropping wagons with a delightful disregard for time. The dock at Granborough, seen here in 1935, was an important cattle-loading-point for the area and was used long after the departure of passenger services. The crowd of people seen by the level-crossing gates just before the station appears to be a Permanent Way gang.

Photograph: Authors' Collection

## WINSLOW ROAD

Winslow Road, the last station before Verney Junction, shortly before passenger services were withdrawn, in 1936. Goods trains continued to use the line for many years afterwards and track remained in position here as a long siding up to Verney Junction until about 1960. The platforms were generous, the 'up' side buildings being in brick. But Winslow Road never bred any rising suburb. No estate agent ever laid out, or even planned, an estate here. Few, if ever, were the Sunday School treats, unless the children were from the local villages making for Aylesbury or London. Even the *Metroland* guides only made a brief mention of the rural delights. In the lengthy spells between trains, pheasants would perch on the wooden fence by the milk churns, and one could hear the cows chewing in the meadows beside the track. Baker Street, Wembley and Harrow Hill were worlds away.

Photograph: Authors' Collection

## AFTERNOON GOODS FROM VERNEY JUNCTION

Round the curve from Verney comes the afternoon freight train one day in July 1936 in charge of 'K' class Number 115 — one of the most powerful locomotives on the Metropolitan. The 'K' class was based on pre-1914 designs by R.E.L. Maunsell for the old South Eastern Railway. The parts were stored during the War and were subsequently assembled, with some additions, by Armstrong Whitworth and Co. to fresh designs by the Met's Chief Mechanical Engineer, George Hally, in 1924. Much of their work was done on goods trains between Verney Junction and Finchley Road.

Photograph: F. H. Stingemore

### 'MAYFLOWER' TAKES A REST

An unusual picture of 'Mayflower' in the late 1920s. The Pullman car may have been parked here awaiting some minor repair or for transfer to Neasden for routine overhaul. The Neasden works carried a full range of Pullman spares for 'Mayflower, 'Galatea' and the Rothschild Saloon. One day an over-energetic employee playing football during the lunch break put the ball through one of the Pullman's oval lights. A complete replacement window was fitted within half an hour so that the car could make its scheduled run between Baker Street and Verney Junction. The end doors were never used, as the Metropolitan did not run corridor stock. A Pullman train was stabled at Verney overnight during the week and was the first 'up' passenger train in the morning. The first passenger was normally Sir Harry Verney, who boarded at Granborough Road. But even Metropolitan Railway directors had to wait for their coffee and hot toast until Quainton Road, where the attendant came on.

Photograph: H.C. Casserley Collection

## THE OUTERMOST FRONTIER

In the bay platform the train to Baker Street waits, while an L.M.S. train for Bletchley has just pulled away from the main line platform. For many years after the closure of the Metropolitan to Verney, the lines were left in place at least as far as Winslow for the storage of redundant rolling stock. The station house on the right remains today, as do the platforms, but all else has gone in the recent past. Now only the occasional freight train rumbles through to Bicester or Bletchley.

Verney Junction really *was* the outermost frontier of Metro-land. No rows of semi-detached houses and parades of shops ever rose on its fields. Few explorers of Metro-land ever came this far; distance and, even in those days, fares made the trip unattractive. Yet those who did come all the way found it a place of peace and contrast with the busy miles through Middlesex, Hertfordshire and the chalky Chilterns. This was the deep countryside. The elms and the oaks and the hawthorns reached mile after mile across the Midland plain. Here were the endless fields of Buckinghamshire that had been unchanged by progress. And on a summer day when the train had left all you could hear was the sound of the crickets in the trackside grass and the song of what seemed to be all the birds of Buckinghamshire and Oxfordshire. At Verney Junction the Metro-land dream ended.

Photograph: H.C. Casserley Collection

9/1997  10

to Buckingham

to Bletchley

VERNEY JUNCTION

to Leicester

Winslow Road

Grandborough Road

Grendon Underwood Junc

to Chea

L.M.S.

QUAINTON ROAD

High St

Waddesdon Manor

Waddesdon Road

Westcott

AYLESBURY

CHESHAM

Gasworks siding

Stoke Mandeville

Wendover

Kingswood 'branch'

Great Missenden

Wotton

AMERSHAM

ill & Luggershall

Wotton

Chalfont & Latimer

Wood Siding

Ashendon Junction

Chorley Wood &

BRILL

Brickworks siding

Princes Risborough

High Wycombe

THE OXFORD & AYLESBURY TRAMROAD COMPANY

A Home in Metro-land